A Primer for the Gradual
Understanding of Gertrude Stein

Edited by Robert Barlett Haas:

A Primer for the Gradual Understanding of Gertrude
Stein

Reflection on the Atomic Bomb: Volume 1 of the
Previously Uncollected Writings of Gertrude Stein

How Writing Is Written: Volume 2 of the Previously
Uncollected Writings of Gertrude Stein

GERTRUDE STEIN A PRIMER FOR THE GRADUAL UNDERSTANDING OF GERTRUDE STEIN GERTRUDE STEIN A PRIMER FOR THE GRADUAL UNDERSTANDING OF GERTRUDE STEIN GERTRUDE STEIN A PRIMER FOR THE GRADUAL UNDERSTANDING OF GERTRUDE STEIN GERTRUDE STEIN

Edited by
ROBERT BARTLETT HAAS

BLACK SPARROW PRESS · SANTA BARBARA · 1976

Cover photograph courtesy of The Collection of American Literature, Beinecke Rare Book and Manuscript Library, Yale University.

Black Sparrow Press
Box 3993
Santa Barbara, CA
93105

SBN 87685-136-7 (paper)
SBN 87685-137-5 (cloth)

For Thornton Wilder

PREFACE

To my mind Gertrude Stein has not always been fortunate in her biographers (except when she put her hand to it herself) or her explainers, and only a handful of essays (among them Thornton Wilder's and those of Marcel Brion, Ralph Church, Donald Gallup, Georgina Melvin, Donald Sutherland, Virginia Tufte and Dorothy van Ghent) come up to my own notion of what illuminates the character of Gertrude Stein's contribution. For the purpose of this volume I therefore determined to read into the record three little known essays about Gertrude Stein which I think *do* illuminate.

Gertrude Stein Raffel's contribution carries the special stamp of family atmosphere and family reminiscence. My own "interview" preserves the flavor of Gertrude Stein talking about Gertrude Stein, and contains some of the very few explications of her own texts ever given by her. Donald Sutherland's essay extends the territory of his excellent book, *Gertrude Stein: A Biography of Her Work*, to give Gertrude Stein a philosopher's due.

The Little Anthology, the playing out here in miniature of an idea I was working on with Gertrude Stein at the time of her death, attempts to supply the reader with carefully chosen samples of each of the major periods of Gertrude Stein's writings, along with examples of each emerging or recurring style.

To provide the reader with such easy touchstones was something Gertrude Stein herself was never even faintly interested in doing. On the other hand she was enthusiastic and sympathetic about my doing it. Some of the basic work of isolating Gertrude Stein's varied concerns in writing has been subsequently and excellently done by Donald Sutherland and Richard Bridgeman, but as the heroic days of Stein scholarship seem now to be past, and what with the final publication of all her major work, I find it appropriate for me to get correction and closure on my own early scheme by summarizing again what I have come to feel about the writing of Gertrude Stein in this newly distilled primer.

This book is not about Gertrude Stein's politics, religion or private life, but about her *work*—which is, I believe, still radical enough to hold our attention in its own right.

ROBERT BARTLETT HAAS

University of California, Los Angeles

1971

PREFACE

A
TRANSATLANTIC
INTERVIEW
1946

An excerpt from the article "Gertrude Stein Talking—A Transatlantic Interview" printed by the UCLAN *Review, Summer 1962; Spring 1963; and Winter 1964. The circumstances reported there were as follows: "* . . . *just before communication with France was cut off and for a short time after the war closed, Gertrude Stein and I worked together on our favorite project. It was to be a book entitled,* A Primer for the Gradual Understanding of Gertrude Stein. *She was "xited" about the title and the idea.*

It was in preparation for this book that the transatlantic interview came about. Since conversation was, in my opinion, one of Stein's great forms, I believed a substantial sample of her oral pyrotechnics should be included in the Primer. *This was before the time of the tape recorder, and so it was arranged that one of our friends, William S. Sutton, lucky enough to be on military assignment in France, agreed to secure an interview for me. My questions would be mailed to him in Paris (I seem to remember he came all the way to Columbus, Ohio, to talk about it first), he would put them to her, and her answers would be recorded in shorthand and sent to me for the chapter to be called "Gertrude Stein Talking."*

Back in Paris, Sutton wrote me the details. "She agreed to the interview and to having a verbatim transcript made of her remarks. On the afternoons of Saturday and Sunday, 5 and 6 of January 1946, the interview which resulted in the accompanying statements took place, in Miss Stein's apartment at No. 5 rue Christine. Each of the interviews lasted from approximately two till five and were held in a cordial and informal atmosphere . . . it is a pity this material could not

13

have been put on a voice recorder, for no one can know Miss Stein without having sat with her and listened to her positive, almost masculine tone informed with an almost mocking note when it is not charged with an earnest seriousness. Now over 70, she is a woman of unusual mental vigor. To see her now makes one regret not having seen her in her prime."

There was something about it all that must have reminded Gertrude Stein of the 1891 Walt Whitman birthday interview in which the great, grey poet built his own legend, the stenographer discreetly hidden behind a screen. She inscribed the typescript as follows: "To Bobby Haas and his progeny forever. You got a scoop! Always, Gertrude Stein."

A TRANSATLANTIC INTERVIEW 1946

Sherwood Anderson wrote, "For me the work of Gertrude Stein consists in a rebuilding, an entire new recasting of life, in the city of words." Is this an adequate summation of what you are trying to do?

It is and it isn't. The thing was not so simple as all that. In the beginning you must remember that I have always been from my babyhood a liberal reader of all English literature. In San Francisco they had a Mechanics Library. As it happened, it had an uncommonly good collection for an ordinary town, and they had a really marvelously complete Seventeenth and Eighteenth Century English Literature collection, and the early Nineteenth Century. And when I was a youngster I used to spend days and days reading things there, and that was my early contact. And then when I became a scientist and became a psychologist, I was only being a scientist for a while, but I did not really care for science. I then went to England and read Elizabethan plays extensively which were very rich in word value.

Everything I have done has been influenced by Flaubert and Cézanne, and this gave me a new feeling about composition. Up to that time composition had consisted of a central idea, to which everything else was an accompaniment and separate but was not an end in itself, and Cézanne conceived the idea that in composition one thing was as important as another thing. Each part is as important as the whole, and that impressed me enormously, and it impressed me so much that I began to write *Three Lives* under this influence and this idea of composition and I was more interested in composition at that moment, this background of word-system, which had come to me from this reading that I had done. I was obsessed by this idea of composition, and the Negro story ("Melanctha" in *Three Lives*) was a quintessence of it.

You see I tried to convey the idea of each part of a composition being as important as the whole. It was the first time in any language that anyone had used that idea of composition in literature. Henry James had a slight inkling of it and was in some senses a forerunner, while in my case I made it stay on the page quite composed. You see he made it sort of like an atmosphere, and it was

15

not solely the realism of the characters but the realism of the composition which was the important thing, the realism of the composition of my thoughts.

After all, to me one human being is as important as another human being, and you might say that the landscape has the same values, a blade of grass has the same value as a tree. Because the realism of the people who did realism before was a realism of trying to make people real. I was not interested in making the people real but in the essence or, as a painter would call it, value. One cannot live without the other. This was an entirely new idea and had been done a little by the Russians but had not been conceived as a reality until I came along, but I got it largely from Cézanne. Flaubert was there as a theme. He, too, had a little of the feeling about this thing, but they none of them conceived it as an entity, no more than any painter had done other than Cézanne. They all fell down on it, because the supremacy of one interest overcame them, while the Cézanne thing I put into words came in the *Three Lives* and was followed by the *Making of Americans*.

In the *Making of Americans* I began the same thing. In trying to make a history of the world my idea here was to write the life of every individual who could possibly live on the earth. I hoped to realize that ambition. My intention was to cover every possible variety of human type in it. I made endless diagrams of every human being, watching people from windows and so on until I could put down every type of human being that could be on the earth. I wanted each one to have the same value. I was not at all interested in the little or big men but to realize absolutely every variety of human experience that it was possible to have, every type, every style and nuance. I have always had this obsession, and that is why I enjoy talking to every GI. I must know every possible nuance.

Conception of this has to be based on a real feeling for every human being. The surprises of it are endless. Still there are the endless surprises, the combination that you don't expect, the relation of men to character that you do not expect. It never ends. All the time in it you see what I am singling out is that one thing has the same value as another. There are of course people who are more important than others in that they have more importance in the world, but this is not essential, and it ceases to be. I have no sense of difference in this respect, because every human being

16

comprises the combination form. Just as everybody has the vote, including the women, I think children should, because as soon as a child is conscious of itself, then it has to me an existence and has a stake in what happens. Everybody who has that stake has that quality of interest, and in the *Making of Americans* that is what I tried to show.

In writing the *Three Lives* I was not particularly conscious of the question of style. The style which everybody shouted about surprised me. I was only interested in these other things. In the beginning gradually I became more conscious of the way you did this thing and I became gradually more conscious of it and at that time particularly of a need for evenness. At this time I threw away punctuation. My real objection to it was that it threw away this balance that I was trying to get, this evenness of everybody having a vote, and that is the reason I am impatient with punctuation. Finally I got obsessed with these enormously long sentences and long paragraphs. All that was an effort to get this evenness, and this went on until it sort of exhausted itself.

On the *Making of Americans* I had written about one thousand pages, and I finished the thing with a sort of rhapsody at the end. Then I started in to write *Matisse, Picasso, and Gertrude Stein.* You will see in each one of these stories that they began in the character of *Making of Americans,* and then in about the middle of it words began to be for the first time more important than the sentence structure or the paragraphs. Something happened. I mean I felt a need. I had thought this thing out and felt a need of breaking it down and forcing it into little pieces. I felt that I had lost contact with the words in building up these Beethovian passages. I had lost that idea gained in my youth from the Seventeenth Century writers, and the little rhymes that used to run through my head from Shakespeare, who was always a passion, got lost from the overall pattern. I recognized and I recognize (if you look at the *Long Gay Book*) this something else I knew would guide that.

I began to play with words then. I was a little obsessed by words of equal value. Picasso was painting my portrait at that time, and he and I used to talk this thing over endlessly. At this time he had just begun on cubism. And I felt that the thing I got from Cézanne was not the last composition. You had to recognize words had lost their value in the Nineteenth Century, particularly towards the end, they had lost much of their variety, and I felt that

I could not go on, that I had to recapture the value of the individual word, find out what it meant and act within it.

Also the fact that as an American my mind was fresher towards language than the average English mind, as we had more or less renewed the word structure in our language. All through that middle period the interest was with that largely, ending up with *Tender Buttons*. In this I think that there are some of the best uses of words that there are. The movement is simple and holds by little words. I had at the same time a new interest in portraiture. I began then to want to make a more complete picture of each word, and that is when the portrait business started. I wait until each word can intimate some part of each little mannerism. In each one of them I was not satisfied until the whole thing formed, and it is very difficult to put it down, to explain, in words.

While during that middle period I had these two things that were working back to the compositional idea, the idea of portraiture and the idea of the recreation of the word. I took individual words and thought about them until I got their weight and volume complete and put them next to another word, and at this same time I found out very soon that there is no such thing as putting them together without sense. It is impossible to put them together without sense. I made innumerable efforts to make words write without sense and found it impossible. Any human being putting down words had to make sense out of them.

All these things interested me very strongly through the middle years from about after the *Making of Americans* until 1911, leading up to *Tender Buttons*, which was the apex of that. That was the culmination. Then came the war, and through the war I was traveling a great deal.

After the war the form of the thing, the question of the play form, began to interest me very much. I did very little work during the war. As soon as the war was over I settled down and wrote the whole of the *Geography and Plays*. That turned into very strong interest in play form, and then I began to be slowly impressed by the idea of narration.

After all, human beings are interested in two things. They are interested in the reality and interested in telling about it. I had struggled up to that time with the creation of reality, and then I became interested in how you could tell this thing in a way that anybody could understand and at the same time keep true to your values, and the thing bothered me a great deal at that time. I did

18

quite a few plays and portraits, and that ended roughly with the *Four Saints*, 1932. Most of the things that are in the *Useful Knowledge*, including a book of poetry which was not printed, were constant effort, and after that I was beginning the narration consisting in plays at first, ending with the *Four Saints*.

After the *Four Saints* the portrait narration began, and I went back to the form of narration, and at that time I had a certain reputation, no success, but a certain reputation, and I was asked to write a biography, and I said "No." And then as a joke I began to write the *Autobiography of Alice Toklas*, and at that moment I had made a rather interesting discovery. A young French poet had begun to write, and I was asked to translate his poems, and there I made a rather startling discovery that other people's words are quite different from one's own, and that they can not be the result of your internal troubles as a writer. They have a totally different sense than when they are your own words. This solved for me the problem of Shakespeare's sonnets, which are so unlike any of his other work. These may have been his own idea, undoubtedly they were, but the words have none of the violence that exists in any of the poems, in any of the plays. They have a roughness and violence in their juxtaposition which the sonnets do not have, and this brought me to a great deal of illumination of narrative, because most narrative is based not about your opinions but upon someone else's.

Therefore narrative has a different concept than poetry or even exposition, because, you see, the narrative in itself is not what is in your mind but what is in somebody else's. Plays use it less, and so I did a tour de force with the *Autobiography of Alice Toklas*, and when I sent the first half to the agent, they sent back a telegram to see which one of us had written it! But still I had done what I saw, what you do in translation or in a narrative. I had recreated the point of view of somebody else. Therefore the words ran with a certain smoothness. Shakespeare never expressed any feelings of his own in those sonnets. They have too much smoothness. He did not feel "This is my emotion, I will write it down." If it is your own feeling, one's words have a fullness and violence.

Then I became more and more interested in the subject of narration, and my work since this, the bulk of my work since then, has been largely narration, and I had done children's stories. I think *Paris, France* and *Wars I have Seen* are the most successful of this. I thought I had done it in *Everybody's Autobiography*. I worked very hard on that and was often very exhausted, but it is often confused and not clarified. But in *Wars I have Seen* and in *Paris, France,* to my feeling, I have done it more completely.

I have done the narration, because in narration your great problem is the problem of time in telling a story of anybody. And that is why newspaper people never become writers, because they have a false sense of time. They have to consider not the time in which to write but the time in which the newspaper is coming out. Three senses of time to struggle with, the time the event took place, the time they are writing, and the time it has to come out. Their sense of time can not be but false. Hemingway, on account of his newspaper training, has a false sense of time. One will sooner or later get this falsity of time, and that is why newspapers cannot be read later out of their published time.

I found out that in the essence of narration is this problem of time. You have as a person writing, and all the really great narration has it, you have to denude yourself of time so that writing time does not exist. If time exists, your writing is ephemeral. You can have a historical time, but for you the time does not exist, and if you are writing about the present, the time element must cease to exist. I did it unconsciously in the *Autobiography of Alice Toklas,* but I did it consciously in *Everybody's Autobiography* and in the last thing *Wars I have Seen.* In it I described something momentous happening under my eyes and I was able to do it without a great sense of time. There should not be a sense of time, but an existence suspended in time. That is really where I am at the present moment, I am still largely meditating about this sense of time.

Words hold an interest that you never lose, but usually at one moment one is more preoccupied with one thing than another, the parts mould into the whole. The narrative phase began in the middle thirties and has continued to the present time. Anderson was interested in the phase I was going through at the moment that he knew me. The thing that worried him the most was the narrative, and like other writers of that period he had not freed himself from the Nineteenth Century influence. He was sort of a cutout of the old into the new design. This is well illustrated in a little book he wrote about farmers.

20

Will you give an account of the results of your experimentation with writing since your lecture tour in the United States?

This has already been covered. There is one thing that impressed me a good many years ago. The characters in the novels of the Nineteenth Century lived a queer kind of way. That is to say people lived and died by these characters. They took a violent interest in them: the Dickens characters, the George Eliot characters, the Meredith characters. They were more real to the average human being than the people they knew. They were far more real, and they would discuss them and feel for them like people they knew. At the end of the Nineteenth Century that died out. Meredith was the last to produce characters who people felt were alive. In the characters of Henry James this is really very little true, the characters do not live very much. The ensemble lives, but nobody gets excited about the characters.

You see there really has been no real novel writing in that sense in the Twentieth Century. The most creative writings were western stories and detective stories, but these were not enough. The hero was usually a dead man in the beginning of the book, and the rest of it is largely a question of a system, one man's way of doing a thing or Scotland Yard's way. The individual that made the Nineteenth Century live practically does not live in the Twentieth Century, where the individual does not stick out enough for the people reading about him. Take Sherwood Anderson, Hemingway, Fitzgerald, in all these it is the title and the form of the book that you remember rather than the characters in the book. That is the reason that the novel has not been a successful form of the Twentieth Century. Proust did it the best, but he made an old-fashioned thing of it. You take the average novel that is written in America today. No character sticks out, and no women's club gets all het up and excited about the character in the latest novel they read, or very little, surely.

You realize how they did in the Nineteenth Century. People really worried about and felt for these characters. Now, you see, even the cinema doesn't do it for them. A few actors or actresses do, but not the characters they portray. As long as the novel has existed, the characters were dominant. Can you imagine any one today weeping over a character? They get excited about the book

21

but not the character.

This has interested me very much. I think that is the reason why the novel as a form has not been successful in the Twentieth Century. That is why biographies have been more successful than novels. This is due in part to this enormous publicity business. The Duchess of Windsor was a more real person to the public and while the divorce was going on was a more actual person than anyone could create. In the Nineteenth Century no one was played up like that, like the Lindbergh kidnapping really roused people's feelings. Then Eleanor Roosevelt is an actuality more than any character in the Twentieth Century novel ever achieved.

To my mind the novel form has not been a successful affair in the Twentieth Century. There has been nothing that you can honestly call a novel. There has not been one in the Twentieth Century with the possible exception of Proust. That makes the novel scheme quite out of the question. One falls back on the thing like I did in *Ida,* where you try to handle a more or less satirical picture within the individual. No individual that you can conceive can hold their own beside life. There has been so much in recent years. Napoleon was, you might say, an ogre in his time. The common people did not know all the everyday things, did not know him intimately, there was not this enormous publicity. People now know the details of important people's daily life unlike they did in the Nineteenth Century. Then the novel supplied imagination where now you have it in publicity, and this changed the whole cast of the novel. So the novel is not a living form, and people try to get out of the difficulty by essay and short story form, and that is a feeble form at best.

The only serious effort that has been made is the detective story, and in a kind of a way Wallace is the only novelist of the Twentieth Century. He failed in the same way. He created an atmosphere of crime and did not have characters that people worried about. You cannot say that there is a novel of the Twentieth Century. I mean a more or less creative writer has never written anything that could in any reasonable sense of the word be called a novel. I have created a lot of characters, but that is another story.

Have there been any new developments in your attitude toward poetry?

Poetry is understandable, and the best poetry is real. The children's books and some of that in *Tender Buttons* and in some of the children's plays. There have been no new developments in poetry farther than that.

How and when are poetry and prose separate things?

I did that pretty thoroughly in that book of poetry and prose, and since then what poetry I have done has been in the children's books, and that you might call spontaneous poetry, and in *Paris, France* there is quite a bit of it, but that is mainly dealing with children. Somehow or other in war time the only thing that is spontaneously poetic is children. Children themselves are poetry. The poetry of adults in wartime is too intentional. It is too much mixed up with everything else. My poetry was children's poetry, and most of it is very good, and some of it as good as anything I have ever done. *The World is Round* is being included in a new American anthology.

The early book, Tender Buttons, *was written in Spain in 1913 and was Gertrude Stein's first attempt to "express the rhythm of the visible world."* Tender Buttons *was, therefore, to Gertrude Stein's development what the "Demoiselles d'Avignon" was to Picasso's, a key work marked with the enormous struggle of creating a new value.*

The following readings were chosen at random from Tender Buttons *and are followed by Gertrude Stein's verbatim responses.*

A DOG

A little monkey goes like a donkey that means to say that means to say that more sighs last goes. Leave with it. A little monkey goes like a donkey.

23

"A little monkey goes like a donkey . . . " That was an effort to illustrate the movement of a donkey going up a hill, you can see it plainly. "A little monkey goes like a donkey." An effort to make the movement of the donkey, and so the picture hangs complete.

A WHITE HUNTER
A white hunter is nearly crazy.

"A white hunter is nearly crazy." This is an abstract, I mean an abstraction of color. If a hunter is white he looks white, and that gives you a natural feeling that he is crazy, a complete portrait by suggestion, that is what I had in mind to write.

A LITTLE GIRL CALLED PAULINE (excerpt)

A little called anything shows shudders.
Come and say what prints all day. A whole few
watermelon. There is no pope.
No cut in pennies and little dressing and choose
wide soles and little spats really little spices.
A little lace makes boils. This is not true . . . .

"A little called anything shows shudders." This was another attempt to have only enough to describe the movement of one of those old-fashioned automobiles, an old Ford, the movement is like that automobile. This is an account of movement that is not always successful. For the most part it is successful and is rather interesting.

A LITTLE BIT OF A TUMBLER

A shining indication of yellow consists in there
having been more of the same color than could have
been expected when all four were bought. This was
the hope which made the six and seven have no use
for any more places and this necessarily spread
into nothing. Spread into nothing.

I have used this idea in more places. I used to take objects on a table, like a tumbler or any kind of object and try to get the picture of it clear and separate in my mind and create a word relationship between the word and the things seen. "A shining indication of yellow . . ." suggests a tumbler and something in it. " . . . when all four were bought" suggests there were four of them. I try to call to the eye the way it appears by suggestion the way a painter can do it. This is difficult and takes a lot of work and concentration to do it. I want to indicate it without calling in other things. "This was the hope which made the six and seven have no use for any more places . . ." Places bring up a reality. " . . . and this necessarily spread into nothing," which does broken tumbler which is the end of the story.

A   WAIST

A star glide, a single frantic sullenness, a single financial grass greediness.

Object that is in wood. Hold the pine, hold the dark, hold in the rush, make the bottom.

A piece of crystal. A change, in a change that is remarkable there is no reason to say that there was a time.

A woolen object gilded. A country climb is the best disgrace, a couple of practices any of them in order is so left.

"A star glide, a single frantic sullenness, a single financial grass greediness." This was probably an effort to express an emotion, another version of an "Ode to a Mistress's Eyebrows." "Object that is in wood. Hold the pine, hold the dark, hold in the rush, make the bottom. A piece of crystal. A change, in a change that is remarkable there is no reason to say that there was a time." This is fairly successful of what I knew up to that date. I did not have to call in other things to help. I do not like to do this, there is so much one must reject to keep the even smoothness of suggestion.

25

A PIECE OF COFFEE

More of double.

A place in no new table.

A single image is not splendor. Dirty is yellow. A sign of more in not mentioned. A piece of coffee is not a detainer. The resemblance to yellow is dirtier and distincter. The clean mixture is whiter and not coal color, never more coal color than altogether.

The sight of a reason, the same sight slighter, the sight of a simpler negative answer, the same sore sounder, the intention to wishing, the same splendor, the same furniture.

The time to show a message is when too late and later there is no hanging in a blight.

A not torn rose-wood color. If it is not dangerous then a pleasure and more than any other if it is cheap is not cheaper. The amusing side is that the sooner there are no fewer the more certain is the necessity dwindled. Supposing that the case contained rose-wood and a color. Supposing that there was no reason for a distress and more likely for a number, supposing that there was no astonishment, is it not necessary to mingle astonishment.

The settling of stationing cleaning is one way not to shatter scatter and scattering. The one way to use custom is to use soap and silk for cleaning. The one way to see cotton is to have a design concentrating the illusion and the illustration. The perfect way is to accustom the thing to have a lining and the shape of a ribbon and to be solid, quite solid in standing and to use heaviness in morning. It is light enough in that. It has that shape nicely. Very nicely may not be exaggerating. Very strongly may be sincerely fainting. May be strangely flattering. May not be strange in everything. May not be strange to.

"Dirty is yellow." Dirty has an association and is a word that I would not use now. I would not use words that have definite associations. This was earlier work and none of the later things have this. This early work is not so successful. It is an effort and does not come clean. "The time to show a message is when too late and later there is no hanging in a blight." There is too much phantasy here. "A not torn rose-wood color. If it . . . is not necessary to mingle astonishment." That is the image but it is not completely successful, but it is better than the first part. You see there is too much appeal to the eye.

"The settling of stationing . . . May not be strange to." There is too much effort. If an effort that you make is successful, if you do get what you want to create, the effort must not show. It should create a satisfaction in the mind of the reader but in the same image as the creation. In this the mind is distracted and that is not satisfactory and it is therefore a failure. Here I am groping. I have not mastered my material. Insofar as creation is successful a reader realizes it as a successful entity, and in this you can see how successfully you have mastered your material.

A BROWN

A brown which is not liquid not more so is relaxed and yet there is a change, a news is pressing.

"A brown which is not liquid . . . " The color is held within and there you see I was groping for the color.

PEELED PENCIL, CHOKE
Rub her coke.

That is where I was beginning and went on a gool deal after that period to make sound pictures but I gave that up as uninteresting.

EGGS

Kind height, kind in the right stomach with a little sudden mill.
Cunning shawl, cunning shawl to be steady.

> *In white in white handkerchiefs with little dots*
> *in a white belt all shadows are singular they are*
> *singular and procured and relieved.*
> *No that is not the cows shame and a precocious*
> *sound, it is a bite.*
> *Cut up alone the paved way which is harm.*
> *Harm is old boat and a likely dash.*

"In white in white handkerchiefs with little dots in a white belt all shadows are singular . . . " There I used a lot of imagery and from what I was interested in it is not a success. It should allow imagery with it without troubling anybody.

SUGAR (excerpts)

> *A violent luck and a whole sample and even then*
> *quiet.*
> *Water is squeezing, water is almost squeezing on*
> *lard. Water, water is a mountain and it is selected*
> *and it is so practical that there is no use in money.*
> *A mind under is exact and so it is necessary to have*
> *a mouth and eye glasses.*
> *A question of sudden rises and more time than*
> *awfulness is so easy and shady. There is precisely*
> *that noise . . . .*
> *Put it in the stew, put it to shame. A little slight*
> *shadow and a solid fine furnace.*
> *The teasing is tender and trying and thought-*
> *ful . .*
> *A canoe is orderly. A period is solemn. A cow*
> *is accepted. . . .*

This is rather fine, looking at it dispassionately. "A violent luck . . . There is precisely that noise." I call that from my standpoint a successful poem. " . . . slight shadow and a solid fine furnace." You see a "little slight shadow" has poetical appeal, but it is not quite successful poetry.

"Water is squeezing, water is almost squeezing on lard." The imagery of that is really a perfect example of realism, there is

28

enough there to a person looking at water that is realistic, there is enough use that is outside the image before your eyes. "A mind under is exact and so it is necessary to have a mouth and eyeglasses." That impresses any person, so to speak it is part of the water and is therefore valid. It is supposed to continue the actual realism of water, of a great body of water.

You must remember each time I took something, I said, I have got to satisfy each realistic thing I feel about it. Looking at your shoe, for instance, I would try to make a complete realistic picture of your shoe. It is devilish difficult and needs perfect concentration, you have to refuse so much and so much intrudes itself upon you that you do not want it, it is exhausting work.

MUTTONS (excerpts)

Mouse and mountain and a quiver, a quaint statue and pain in an exterior and silence more silence louder shows salmon a mischief intender . . . A sign is the specimen spoken.

A meal in mutton, mutton, why is lamb cheaper, it is cheaper because so little is more. Lecture, lecture and repeat instruction.

"Mouse and mountain and a quiver . . . " Here you see I was wise enough not to hesitate and still I dominated. " . . . A sign is the specimen spoken." You see also here you have a very good example. You take a paragraph like that and the values are pretty steady though this seems difficult to a normal reader's understanding. This is pretty good because it is more abstract.

You see it is the people who generally smell of the museums who are accepted, and it is the new who are not accepted. You have got to accept a complete difference. It is hard to accept that, it is much easier to have one hand in the past. That is why James Joyce was accepted and I was not. He leaned toward the past, in my work the newness and difference is fundamental. Cézanne was my great influence though I never met him; he was an ailing man at that time.

This book is interesting as there is as much failure as success in

29

it. When this was printed I did not understand this creation. I can see now, but one cannot understand a thing until it is done. With a thing in the process of doing, you do not know what you are doing until it is done, finished, and thus you cannot explain it. Until then you are struggling.

I was not interested in what people would think when they read this poetry; I was entirely taken up with my problem and if it did not tell my story it would tell some story. They might have another conception which would be their affair. It is not necessarily attached to the original idea I had when I wrote it.

Nobody enters into the mind of someone else, not even a husband and wife. You may touch, but you do not enter into each other's mind. Why should you? In a created thing it means more to the writer than it means to the reader. It can only mean something to one person and that person the one who wrote it.

What was the character of your first audience?

Well, Carl Van Vechten was the first person who published me, and Carl was a great believer in me from the very beginning. Then there was a group of young people in New York. I do not know what has become of them now. They were all friends of Carl Van Vechten. There was a man called Don Marquis, and he in the guise of making fun was very much interested in my work. Henry McBride said, "If you laugh with her you have more fun than laughing at her." Protestingly, he used pieces of my work in his paper. I was essentially a writer's writer. My audience in France, that was a perfect audience. The first person who ever printed anything of mine here was Jean Cocteau. That was in a book called *Potomac*, in 1913. He was the first one. He printed the *Portrait of Mabel Dodge*, which he heard read in a cafe. Then there was Edith Sitwell, who was my chief English contact. Harold Acton was another one. Then there was Bernard Fay, who printed a piece of *Melanctha*, and he lectured on my work a great deal at the Collège de France.

Will you trace for me something of the nature of the development of your acceptance?

30

I became fairly early in the game a writer's writer. Sherwood Anderson and people like that scattered all over the country were interested, and it gave them something to think about—Bromfield, Hemingway, Anderson, Wendell Wilcox—and it disseminated between one and another. When I was at a dinner party at Beverly Hills in Hollywood, there were a great many of the big vedettes of the cinema. After the dinner all these people were seated in front of me, and I did not know what it was all about or what they wanted, and finally one blurted out, "What we want to know is how do you get so much publicity?" So I told them, "By having such a small audience. Begin with a small audience. If that small audience really believes, they make a big noise, and a big audience does not make a noise at all."

What is your attitude toward lecturing?

Picasso and I were talking the other day. I always said I never minded living in France. I write with my eyes, not with my ears or mouth. I hate lecturing, because you begin to hear yourself talk, because sooner or later you hear your voice, and you do not hear what you say. You just hear what they hear you say. As a matter of fact, as a writer I write entirely with my eyes. The words as seen by my eyes are the important words, and the ears and mouth do not count. I said to Picasso, "When you were a kid you never looked at things." He seemed to swallow the things he saw but he never looked, and I said, "In recent years you have been looking, you see too much, it is a mistake for you." He said, "You are quite right." A writer should write with his eyes, and a painter paint with his ears. You should always paint knowledge which you have acquired, not by looking but by swallowing. I have always noticed that in portraits of really great writers the mouth is always firmly closed.

What about your relationship with Richard Wright?

Richard Wright I first encountered through his writings on my work. I was impressed by the quality of his writings. I think in the first place he has a great mastery of the English language, and I think, to my mind, he has succeeded in doing the most creative work that has been done in many a year. His *Black Boy* is a very masterly novel, and every time he writes there is a form. He dominates his language. He holds it. *Uncle Tom's Children* has a piece of consummate description in the first of the story. I do not think there has been anything done like it since I wrote *Three Lives*. There has not been anything so good in the English language since. The others are merely followers. Richard Wright is not a follower. He does admire my writing thoroughly. He did a criticism of *Wars I Have Seen*. I saw it in a newspaper and was astounded by the quality of the writing and asked who he was and was given some of his books. He writes very wonderful letters. His meditations on the American scene are the most interesting I have heard from anybody. I think he is a very, very interesting person.

In Esquire, *July 1945, Sinclair Lewis wrote: " . . . When the exhibitionist deliberately makes his rites as confusing as possible, he is permitted to go on only because so many people are afraid to blurt out, 'I don't know what it means.' For that same reason, Gertrude Stein, the Mother Superior of all that shoddy magic, is still extensively admired even though she is also extensively unread."*

The best answer to that is what Picasso said, a perfectly good answer. In the first place this is my answer. The facts of the case are that all these people, including myself, are people with a considerably large endowment, and most of us spent thirty years of our life in being made fun of and laughed at and criticized and having no existence and being without a cent of income. The work needs concentration, and one is often exhausted by it. No one would do this merely for exhibitionism; there is too much bitterness. Picasso said, "You see, the situation is very simple. Anybody that creates a new thing has to make it ugly. The effort of creation is so great, that trying to get away from the other things, the contemporary insistence, is so great that the effort to break it gives the appearance of ugliness. Your followers can make it pretty, so generally followers are accepted before the master. The master has the stain of ugliness. The followers who make it pretty are accepted. The people then go back to the original. They see the beauty and bring it back to the original."

Sinclair Lewis would never accept, for instance, that the GI is an entirely different creature from the Sammy of the last war. It would never occur to him to enter into things. He follows the journalistic form and is a newspaperman with a gift for writing books. I have been accused of repetition, but that is not so, and Sinclair Lewis is talking as they talked thirty years ago. The young man and the GI of today would never come to talk to me if I was an exhibitionist or a repetitionist, because time would have killed that. These do not last through time. The point is that the repetition is in Lewis; it is not in me. Lewis is saying what they said thirty years ago about *Tender Buttons*. Anderson also was protesting against it. You see the thing I mean is very well stated in *Composition*. I do not consider that any creative artist is anything but contemporary. Only he is sensitive to what is contemporary long before the average human being is. He puts down what is contemporary, and it is exactly that. Sooner or later people realize it.

I remember one day in the rue Raspail I was walking with Picasso. There came down the street a camouflaged truck, and he stood absolutely still and stared at it and said, "That is what you and I have been doing for years. What is the matter with these people?" He had known fifteen years before they knew that it was contemporary. Picasso said that no one is capable of understanding you who is not capable of doing the same work himself.

Why have you not explained more generally what you are attempting to do?

You explain it to anybody that asks, but if the asking desire is not there, the explanation is useless. You can explain when there is contact, and that person who has made contact can explain to others. It is in *Wars I Have Seen* and *Everybody's Autobiography*. But the thing you have to remember is that it is what these people like, and what Sinclair Lewis cannot understand is that it lives and is ageless.

He is the perfect example of the false sense of time of the newspaper world. He lives in the past and present and not the future. They have no time other than false time. He makes *Main Street* as if time were the main thing, which it isn't. He does not see that

Main Street is made up of clear accounts of things. He was always dominated by an artificial time when he wrote *Main Street*. After all, the average human being is selfish and as such is interesting, everybody is, and he gives a little character to it. All right, but that is a cliché. He did not create actual human beings at any time. That is what makes it newspaper. Sinclair Lewis is the typical newspaperman who writes novels as a newspaperman, and everything he says is newspaper. The difference between a thinker and a newspaperman is that a thinker enters right into things; a newspaperman is superficial.

When I was in America one day there were three young newspapermen and a photographer, and they had just come out of college and took themselvse very seriously, but eventually we got talking about things in general. The only one of the four of them who understood my writing was the photographer. He said, "I don't have to remember what you say. I am not involved with the mechanics of remembering it, and so I can understand it. They are too busy trying to remember what you say."

Why did you answer questionnaires like those in Little Review *and* transition *cryptically, with a chip on your shoulder?*

That does not interest me; it is like the Gallup Poll. After all, my only thought is a complicated simplicity. I like a thing simple, but it must be simple through complication. Everything must come into your scheme; otherwise you cannot achieve real simplicity. A great deal of this I owe to a great teacher, William James. He said, "Never reject anything. Nothing has been proved. If you reject anything, that is the beginning of the end as an intellectual." He was my big influence when I was at college. He was a man who always said, "Complicate your life as much as you please, it has got to simplify."

Nothing can be the same thing to the other person. Nobody can enter into anybody else's mind; so why try? One can only enter into it in a superficial way. You have slight contacts with other people's minds, but you cannot enter into them.

34

Then why did you publish manuscripts that were really written only for yourself?

There is the eternal vanity of the mind. One wants to see one's children in the world and have them admired like any fond parent, and it is a bitter blow to have them refused or mocked. It is just as bitter for me to have a thing refused as for any little writer with his first manuscript. Anything you create you want to exist, and its means of existence is in being printed.

A LITTLE ANTHOLOGY
OF GERTRUDE STEIN—1895-1946

Radcliffe Themes (1895)

Gertrude Stein's college themes show little promise of the great innovative writer she was later to become. Rosalind Miller's Gertrude Stein: Form and Intelligibility *(1949) made them available for the first time. Richard Bridgeman* (Gertrude Stein in Pieces, p. 5) *has dealt with them by analyzing in detail the writing problems: "They affected her spelling, her syntax, her tone, and her logic, and she was never entirely cured of them."*

She developed few of the writer's conventional controls as a student of William Vaughan Moody. And yet, in less than a decade, this fiercely independent, ineffectively expressive girl had given up a career in medicine, gone to live permanently in Europe, and finished the manuscript of a book, Things as They Are *(1903) in which Bridgeman (p. 45) concedes her now "able to express the subtlety of human behavior within a controlled framework."*

Somehow, with the turn of the century, she had found her métier.

April 25, 1895

> His life is gentle and the elements
> So mix'd in him, that Nature might stand up
> And say to all the world, "this is a man."

Is life worth living? Yes, a thousand times yes when the world still holds such spirits as Prof. James. He is truly a man among men; a scientist of force and originality embodying all that is strongest and worthiest in the scientific spirit; a metaphysician skilled in abstract thought, clear and vigorous and yet too great to worship logic as his God, and narrow himself to a belief merely in the reason of man.

A man he is who has lived sympathetically not alone all thought but all life. He stands firmly, nobly for the dignity of man. His faith is not that of a cringing coward before an all-powerful master, but of a strong man willing to fight, to suffer and endure. He has not accepted faith because it is easy and pleasing. He has thought and lived many years and at last says with a voice of authority, if life does not mean this, I don't know what it means.

What can one say more? He is a strong sane noble personality reacting truly on all experience that life has given him. He is a man take him for all in all.

April 26, 1895

"A new boarder is coming," said our landlady the other day at the table. "A new boarder we don't want any new boarders" we the family decided in a private meeting called to get opinions on this important question. We had nothing to say, however, and the new boarder has come.

The first night she swept in with a royal air and we were all awe-struck. She condescendingly bowed to us poor plebians and then majestically seated herself. Miss Harriet who used to do all the talking was suddenly strangely silent. At last she picked up her courage and ventured a remark. The new boarder condescended to answer her. We breathed more freely and admired Miss Harriet and wished we could do it too.

Then the new boarder began to talk. She talks all the time now (and we are all crushed to earth never to rise again). Whenever we venture an opinion she rises in her majesty, tells us of some great man who believes as she does and has told her so and we meekly retire.

She seems to have known all the great people since the time of Adam and they have all given her their private views on all subjects. Our landlady looks at her, drinking her in with open mouth, eyes and ears. She gives her a finger-bowl at dinner too and we poor plebe look on in envy and can only hope that some day we too will know some great man.

Narrative as Process (1903-1912)

Three major works fall into this period: Things as They Are *(1903)* Three Lives *(1905-1906), and* The Making of Americans *(1906-1911) a monumental book of a thousand printed pages which begins in the style of the others but ends in a new one.*

Of the first two books it may be said that stylistically they were written under the influence of William James, the psychologist and philosopher. James proved to be Gertrude Stein's most stimulating teacher while she was at Radcliffe. His interest in the inner workings of the human mind led her first to consider a career in science, but later to apply his theories in literature. The result was an inner-oriented form of composition in which the traditional telling by chronological narrative was of less interest to Gertrude Stein than was the discovery of a prose style which would enable her to mirror either the speech of her characters as she perceived it, or their mental processes, or her own responses as she sought to grasp "basic natures" and struggled to find a way to externalize in words, and with exactitude, all these very internal states. Readers of Henry James, particularly of The Europeans, *or even* Washington Square, *will recognize the literary springboard if not the literary fulfillment of this approach.*

The Making of Americans *begins as a chronological narrative, progresses through a vast number of psychological portraits of individuals (in which Gertrude Stein's own subjective processes are reflected) and ends in an elevated style which Bridgeman (p. 98) aptly describes as being built from*

43

"a simplified, abstract and repeated vocabulary, and utilizing participles, gerunds and impersonal pronouns moving with maddening deliberateness through diagrammatic sentences."

All three of these manners are present in "Ada", a portrait of Alice B. Toklas, written before 1912. The very pale chronological narrative tells of a young woman whose mother dies and who then becomes unhappy, decides to leave home, finds happiness again in another setting. The all encompassing process style presents the writer's characterization of Ada through an accumulation of specific psychological detail, as well as through the progressive shaping of this subjective material (with all the fits and starts, randomness, repetitions and unexpected revelations which characterize the workings of the human mind) into a final distinctive composition. The third style may be found in the last paragraph only.

ADA

Barnes Colhard did not say he would not do it but he did not do it. He did it and then he did not do it, he did not ever think about it. He just thought some time he might do something.

His father Mr. Abram Colhard spoke about it to every one and very many of them spoke to Barnes Colhard about it and he always listened to them.

Then Barnes fell in love with a very nice girl and she would not marry him. He cried then, his father Mr. Abram Colhard comforted him and they took a trip and Barnes promised he would do what his father wanted him to be doing. He did not do the thing, he thought he would do another thing, he did not do the other thing, his father Mr. Colhard did not want him to do the other thing. He really did not do anything then. When he was a good deal older he married a very rich girl. He had thought perhaps he would not propose to her but his sister wrote to him that it would be a good thing. He married the rich girl and she thought he was the most wonderful man and one who knew everything. Barnes never spent more than the income of the fortune he and his wife had then, that is to say they did not spend more than the income and this was a surprise to very many who knew about him and about his marrying the girl who had such a large fortune. He had a happy life while he was living and after he was dead his wife and children remembered him.

He had a sister who also was successful enough in being one being living. His sister was one who came to be happier than most people come to be in living. She came to be a completely happy one. She was twice as old as her brother. She had been a very good daughter to her mother. She and her mother had always told very pretty stories to each other. Many old men loved to hear her tell these stories to her mother. Every one who ever knew her mother liked her mother. Many were sorry later than not every one liked the daughter. Many did like the daughter but not every one as every one had liked the mother. The daughter was charming inside in her, it did not show outside in her to everyone, it certainly did to some. She did sometimes think her mother would be pleased with a story that did not please her mother, when her mother later was sicker the daughter knew that there were some stories she could tell her that would not please her mother. Her mother died and really mostly altogether the mother and the daughter had told each stories very happily together.

The daughter then kept house for her father and took care of her brother. There were many relations who lived with them. The daughter did not like them to live with them and she did not like them to die with them. The daughter, Ada they had called her after her grandmother who had delightful ways of smelling flowers and eating dates and sugar, did not like it at all then as she did not like so much dying and she did not like any of the living she was doing then. Every now and then some old gentleman told delightful stories to her. Mostly then there were not nice stories told by any one then in her living. She told her father Mr. Abram Colhard that she did not like it at all being one being living then. He never said anything. She was afraid then, she was one needing charming stories and happy telling of them and not having that thing she was always trembling. Then every one who could live with them were dead and there were then the father and the son a young man then and the daughter coming to be that one then. Her grandfather had left some money to them each one of them. Ada said she was going to use it to go away from them. The father said nothing then, then he said something and she said nothing then, then they both said nothing and then it was that she went away from them. The father was quite tender then, she was his daughter then. He wrote her tender letters then, she wrote him tender letters then, she never went back to live with him. He wanted her to come and she wrote him tender letters then. He liked the tender letters she wrote to him. He wanted her to live with him. She answered him by writing tender letters to him and telling very nice stories indeed in them. He wrote nothing and then he wrote again and there was some waiting and then he wrote tender letters again and again.

She came to be happier than anybody else who was living then. It is easy to believe this thing. She was telling some one, who was loving every story that was charming. Some one who was living was almost always listening. Some one who was loving was almost always listening. That one who was loving was almost always listening. That one who was loving was telling about being one then listening. That one being loving was then telling stories having a beginning and a middle and an ending. That one was then one always completely listening. Ada was then one and all her living then one completely telling stories that were charming, completely

46

listening to stories having a beginning and a middle and an ending. Trembling was all living, living was all loving, some one was then the other one. Certainly this one was loving this Ada then. And certainly Ada all her living then was happier in living than any one else who ever could, who was, who is, who ever will be living.

Use of the Continuous Present

The concluding paragraph of "Ada" samples a style in which Gertrude Stein carries the Jamesian notion of dynamic perception to another level of complexity. The awareness of internal states, which led Gertrude Stein away from traditional historical narrative in her writing and to the redefinition of narrative as internal process, was further elaborated by William James in his theories of knowledge, experience and reality. Knowledge, James held, is what you know; and all knowledge (whether of the present or the past) is held within the experience of the present. This is what is real. Reality is now, and this present is in continual flux.

As applied by Gertrude Stein in aesthetic theory, writing, to be "real", must be a description of the "now". The past as past could thus no longer be the content of her writing. Goodbye history. Goodbye traditional narrative which employed a beginning, a middle and an ending. Goodbye remembered events, resemblances, types and other remembered forms. Goodbye repetition, in the mechanical sense. Goodbye past tense.

Now the prose takes on a cinematic style. Each statement made is uniquely felt, uniquely formed in the present, and is succeeded by another, slightly different, like the successive frames of a film that build an image which seems to prolong itself in the present for a given period of time.

This is the style of great portions of The Making of Americans, *but particularly the concluding section; of much of* A Long Gay Book *(1909-1912)*, Two: Gertrude Stein and Her

Brother *(1910-1912)*, Matisse, Picasso and Gertrude Stein *(1911-1912) and of many portraits of the 1908-1912 period, as well as of subsequent writings in this recurring "participial" style.*

A complete portrait using the device of the continuous present is "Picasso" (1909). The basis of the style has been characterized by Donald Sutherland (p. 174) as "the isolation of present internal time."

PICASSO

One whom some were certainly following was one who was completely charming. One whom some were certainly following was one who was charming. One whom some were following was one who was completely charming. One whom some were following was one who was completely charming.

Some were certainly following and were certain that the one they were following was one working and was one bringing out of himself then something. Some were certainly following and were certain that the one they were then following was one bringing out of himself then something that was coming to be a heavy thing, a solid thing and a complete thing.

One whom some were certainly following was one working and certainly was one bringing something out of himself then and was one who had been all his living had been one having something coming out of him.

Something had been coming out of him, certainly it had been coming out of him, certainly it was something, certainly it had been coming out of him and it had meaning, a charming meaning, a solid meaning, a struggling meaning, a clear meaning.

One whom some were certainly following and some were certainly following him, one whom some were certainly following was one certainly working.

One whom some were certainly following was one having something coming out of him something having meaning and this one was certainly working then.

This one was working and something was coming then, something was coming out of this one then. This one was one and always there was something coming out of this one and always there had been something coming out of this one. This one had never been one not having something coming out of this one. This one was one having something coming out of this one. This one had been one whom some were following. This one was one whom some were following. This one was being one whom some were following. This one was one who was working.

This one was one who was working. This one was one being one having something being coming out of him. This one was one going on having something come out of him. This one was one

51

going on working. This one was one whom some were following. This one was one who was working.

This one always had something being coming out of this one. This one was working. This one always had been working. This one was always having something that was coming out of this one that was a solid thing, a charming thing, a lovely thing, a perplexing thing, a disconcerting thing, a simple thing, a clear thing, a complicated thing, an interesting thing, a disturbing thing, a repellant thing, a very pretty thing. This one was one certainly being one having something coming out of him. This one was one whom some were following. This one was one who was working.

This one was one who was working and certainly this one was needing to be working so as to be one being working. This one was one having something coming out of him. This one would be one all his living having something coming out of him. This one was working and then this one was working and this one was needing to be working, not to be one having something coming out of him something having meaning, but was needing to be working so as to be one working.

This one was certainly working and working was something this one was certain this one would be doing and this one was doing that thing, this one was working. This one was not one completely working. This one was not ever completely working. This one certainly was not completely working.

This one was one having always something being coming out of him, something having completely a real meaning. This one was one whom some were following. This one was one who was working. This one was one who was working and he was one needing this thing needing to be working so as to be one having some way of being one having some way of working. This one was one who was working. This one was one having something come out of him something having meaning. This one was one always having something come out of him and this thing the thing coming out of him always had real meaning. This one was one who was working. This one was one who was almost always working. This one was not one completely working. This one was one not ever completely working. This one was not one working to have anything come out of him. This one did have something having meaning that did come out of him. He always did have something come out of him. He was working, he was not ever completely working. He did have

52

some following. They were always following him. Some were certainly following him. He was one who was working. He was one having something coming out of him something having meaning. He was not ever completely working.

Direct Description: The Visible World (1913)

In what has been called her "Spanish Period", Gertrude Stein undertook an even more radical change of style. "The business of Art," she says in Composition as Explanation *(1926), "is to live in the actual present, that is the complete actual present, and to express that complete actual present." What is the character of this reality, this "complete actual present"?*

Kallen (pp. 37-38) describes it thus: "Suppose you take the world as it comes. Suppose you take the world at its face value. Then reality is what you know it as. You find the substantive parts of it connected by relations as truly present and existent as the parts themselves. You find transition and change, continuity and discontinuity, routine and surprise, multiple unities of manifold kinds, realities of various stuffs and powers, all connected with one another by transitions from next to next, each standing away, alone, unmitigated, unincludable, now from some things, now from others. You find movement. You find beginnings, you find endings, you find continuity and you find transformation. In a word, the world of the daily life which we touch and see and hear and smell and taste, which we struggle against and work together with, need be none other than we experience it to be . . ."

And how does one describe this reality of flux and change, inner and outer, of parts and relationships, of routine and surprise? For Gertrude Stein the answer at this stage lay in giving up one more convention of writing—Aristotelian language patterns, or the language which emphasizes the static— for a language which emphasizes the process character of

55

nature and its vivid moment-to-moment novelty.

The language which might express the "complete actual present" in all its complexity of texture and quality was the language of direct description—*a language in which meaning "leaps gaps, indifferent to normal transitions," as* Bridgeman *(pp. 57-58) puts it, and which yields not the conventional "sense" but rather "a perpetually valid description" of the flux of reality, a "spontaneous composition [seen] as living in the present at the front end of time."*

Gertrude Stein practiced this non-discursive kind of writing as early as 1911. The key work in this style is Tender Buttons *(1913), Gertrude Stein's systematic, concentrated description of the visible world of objects, food and rooms in direct, spontaneous, fluid and multi-oriented language. Glimmers of it had appeared in the last pages of* A Long Gay Book. *The approach was later used to describe people, places and crowds. It was the composition of "using everything, beginning again and again", as she wrote in* Composition as Explanation; *she describes the process again in* Lectures in America *(1934) and in the* Transatlantic Interview *(1946).*

A brief work in direct description is "Susie Asado" (1913), Gertrude Stein's poetic portrait of a Spanish dancer. A longer prose example in which she tried to capture the "rhythm of the visible world" is "Mabel Dodge at the Villa Curonia" (1911) written during a stay in Florence.

The particular alchemy by which she catches the texture of the "complete actual present" in these pieces is very personal indeed. The "meaning" of the work lay for Gertrude Stein in the degree of exactitude, or the literalness, with which she was able to describe the particular segment of "reality" which held her attention. Her theory of communication was, simply, that minds can never meet, only touch, so the reader was expected to take the results on faith.

The responsibility of the artist was not to the reader but to the exactitude of description as Gertrude Stein perceived it (Everybody's Autobiography, p. 267) " . . . *one must realize what there is inside in one and then in some way it comes into words and the more exactly the words fit the emotion the more beautiful the words that is what does happen* . . . " .

SUSIE ASADO

Sweet sweet sweet sweet sweet tea.
    Susie Asado.
Sweet sweet sweet sweet sweet tea.
    Susie Asado.
Susie Asado which is a told tray sure.
A lean on the shoe this means slips slips hers.
When the ancient light grey is clean it is yellow, it is a silver seller.
This is a please this is a please there are the saids to jelly. These are the wets these say the sets to leave a crown to Incy.
Incy is short for incubus.
A pot. A pot is a beginning of a rare bit of trees. Trees tremble. the old vats are in bobbles, bobbles which shade and shove and render clean, render clean must.
    Drink pups.
Drinks pups drink pups lease a sash hold, see it shine and a bobolink has pins. It shows a nail.
What is a nail. A nail is unison.
Sweet sweet sweet sweet sweet tea.

PORTRAIT OF MABEL DODGE AT THE VILLA CURONIA

The days are wonderful and the nights are wonderful and the life is pleasant.

Bargaining is something and there is not that success. The intention is what if application has that accident results are reappearing. They did not darken. That was not an adulteration.

So much breathing has not the same place when there is that much beginning. So much breathing has not the same place when the ending is lessening. So much breathing has the same place and there must not be so much suggestion. There can be there the habit that there is if there is no need of resting. The absence is not alternative.

Any time is the half of all the noise and there is not that disappointment. There is no distraction. An argument is clear.

Packing is not the same when the place which has all that is not emptied. There came there the hall and this was not the establishment. It had not all the meaning.

Blankets are warmer in the summer and the winter is not lonely. This does not assure the forgetting of the intention when there has been and there is every way to send some. There does not happen to be a dislike for water. This is not heartening.

As the expedition is without the participation of the question there will be nicely all that energy. They can arrange that the little color is not bestowed. They can leave it in regaining that intention. It is mostly repaid. There can be an irrigation. They can have the whole paper and they send it in some package. It is not inundated.

A bottle that has all the time to stand open is not so clearly shown when there is green color there. This is not the only way to change it. A little raw potato and then all that softer does happen to show that there has been enough. It changes the expression.

It is not darker and the present time is the best time to agree. This which has been feeling is what has the appetite and the patience and the time to stay. This is not collaborating.

All the attention is when there is not enough to do. This does not determine a question. The only reason that there is not that pressure is that there is a suggestion. There are many going. A delight is not bent. There had been that little wagon. There is that precision when there has not been an imagination. There has not been that

58

kind abandonment. Nobody is alone. If the spread that is not a piece removed from the bed is likely to be whiter then certainly the sprinkling is not drying. There can be the message where the print is pasted and this does not mean that there is that esteem. There can be the likelihood of all the days not coming later and this will not deepen the collected dim version.

It is a gnarled division that which is not any obstruction and the forgotten swelling is certainly attracting, it is attracting the whiter division, it is not sinking to be growing, it is not darkening to be disappearing, it is not aged to be annoying. There can not be sighing. This is this bliss.

Not to be wrapped and then to forget undertaking, the credit and then the resting of that interval, the pressing of the sounding when there is no trinket is not altering, there can be pleasing classing clothing.

A sap that is that adaptation is the drinking that is not increasing. There can be that lack of quivering. That does not originate every invitation. There is not wedding introduction. There is not all that filling. There is the climate that is not existing there is that plainer. There is the likeliness lying in liking likely likeliness. There is that dispensation. There is the paling that is not reddening, there is the reddening that is not reddening, there is that protection, there is that destruction, there is not the present lessening there is the argument of increasing. There is that that is not that which is that resting. There is not that occupation. There is that particular half of directing that there is that particular whole direction that is not all the measure of any combination. Gliding is not heavily moving. Looking is not vanishing. Laughing is not evaporating. There can be the climax. There can be the same dress. There can be an old dress. There can be the way there is that way there is that which is not that charging what is a regular way of paying. There has been William. All the time is likely. There is the condition. There has been admitting. There is not the print. There is that smiling. There is the season. There is that where there is not that which is where there is what there is which is beguiling. There is a paste.

Abandon a garden and the house is bigger. This is not smiling. This is comfortable. There is the comforting of predilection. An open object is establishing the loss that there was when the vase was not inside the place. It was not wandering.

A plank that was dry was not disturbing the smell of burning and altogether there was the best kind of sitting there could never be all the edging that the largest chair was having. It was not pushed. It moved then. There was not that lifting. There was that which was not any contradiction and there was not the bland fight that did not have that regulation. The contents were not darkening. There was not that hesitation. It was occupied. That was not occupying any exception. Any one had come. There was that distribution.

There was not that velvet spread when there was a pleasant head. The color was paler. The moving regulating is not a distinction. The place is there.

Likely there is not that departure when the whole place that has that texture is so much in the way. It is not there to stay. It does not change that way. A pressure is not later. There is the same. There is not the shame. There is that pleasure.

In burying that game there is not a change of name. There is not perplexing and co-ordination. The toy that is not round has to be found and looking is not straining such relation. There can be that company. It is not wider when the length is not longer and that does make that way of staying away. Every one is exchanging returning. There is not a prediction. The whole day is that way. Any one is resting to say that the time which is not reverberating is acting in partaking.

A walk that is not stepped where the floor is covered is not in the place where the room is entered. The whole one is the same. There is not any stone. There is the wide door that is narrow on the floor. There is all that place.

There is that desire and there is no pleasure and the place is filling the only space that is placed where all the piling is not adjoining. There is not that distraction.

Praying has intention and relieving that situation is not solemn. There comes that way.

The time that is the smell of the plain season is not showing the water is running. There is not all that breath. There is the use of the stone and there is the place of the stuff and there is the practice of expending questioning. There is not that differentiation. There is that which is in time. There is the room that is the largest place when there is all that is where there is space. There is not that perturbation. The legs that show are not the certain ones that have been used. All legs are used. There is no action meant.

60

The particular space is not beguiling. There is that participation. It is not passing any way. It has that to show. It is why there is no exhalation.

There is all there is when there has all there has where there is what there is. That is what is done when there is done what is done and the union is won and the division is the explicit visit. There is not all of any visit.

Direct Description: The Audible World

Gertrude Stein's work in "The Spanish Period" was very intense and systematic. She wrote (transition, #14, Fall 1923, p. 13), "It was my first conscious struggle with the problem of correlating sight, sound, and sense, and eliminating rhythm . . . " . Tender Buttons had presented direct descriptions of the visual world, each a still life written with a sense of the moment-to-moment uniqueness of each thing that exists and in a language similar in structure to direct experience. Abstraction of the audible aspects of experience may be found in the innumerable plays Gertrude Stein wrote at this time. These were later printed in Geography and Plays *(1922).*

"Ladies' Voices" of 1916 is an excellent example. Narrative is dispensed with as a literary device. Acts and scenes are apparently determined by inner logic. The sound of voices turns and twists in the air: questions are asked, statements are made, attitudes expressed, relationships implied, spoken phrases treasured.

Donald Sutherland (p. 91) says of such writing, " . . . the reality is now the expressive organization, the harmonies or interrelated detail of the work."

LADIES' VOICES

CURTAIN RAISER

Ladies' voices give pleasure.

The acting two is easily lead. Leading is not in winter. Here the winter is sunny.

Does that surprise you.

Ladies voices together and then she came in.

Very well good night.

Very well good night.

(Mrs. Cardillac.)

That's silver.

You mean the sound.

Yes the sound.

ACT II.

Honest to God Miss Williams I don't mean to say that I was older.

But you were.

Yes I was. I do not excuse myself. I feel that there is no reason for passing an archduke.

You like the word.

You know very well that they call it their house.

As Christ was to Lazarus so was the founder of the hill to Mahon.

You really mean it.

I do.

ACT III.

Yes Genevieve does not know it. What. That we are seeing Caesar.

Caesar kisses.

Kisses today.

Caesar kisses every day.

Genevieve does not know that it is only in this country that she could speak as she does.

She does speak very well doesn't she. She told them that there was not the slightest intention on the part of her countrymen to eat the fish that was not caught in their country.

In this she was mistaken.

What are ladies voices.
Do you mean to believe me.
Have you caught the sun.
Dear me have you caught the sun.

SCENE II.

Did you say they were different. I said it made no difference.
Where does it. Yes.
Mr. Richard Sutherland. This is a name I know.
Yes.
The Hotel Victoria.
Many words spoken to me have seemed English.
Yes we do hear one another and yet what are called voices the best decision in telling of balls.
Masked balls.
Yes masked balls.
Poor Augustine.

Direct Description: Movement in Space

Things and people in relation and in movement also pre-occupied Gertrude Stein at this time. Portraits such as "Susie Asado" and "Preciocilla" clearly go in this direction, as do certain expository works such as "Scenes. Actions and Dispositions of Relations and Positions" (1913), "A Curtain Raiser" (1913), "Pink Melon Joy" (1915), "If You Had Three Husbands" (1915), "Advertisements" (1916), and finally lead to the "spectacle plays" of Geography and Plays *and those printed later in* Useful Knowledge *(1928) and* Operas and Plays *(1932).*

The language of the later plays varies from the splintered kaleidoscope style of Tender Buttons *and "Susie Asado" and the telephonic dialoguing of "Ladies' Voices". There are even plays which are primarily portraits. After World War I, the prose smoothes out into a more easygoing, flowing style, as if the rigors of direct description had been weathered and the technique now lay comfortably in the hand of the writer.*

A fascinating and frequently overlooked summary work of this period is "A Movie" (1920) which Gertrude Stein said was about the taxis of the Battle of the Marne and the Allied march through the Arc de Triomphe. Here the time and movement devices of the early film are suggested—the fade-in, the take, the flicker, the close-up, the flash-back, the chase, the obligatory love scene, climax and the heroic finale.

A MOVIE

Eyes are a surprise
Printzess a dream
Buzz is spelled with z
Fuss is spelled with s
So is business.

The UNITED STATES is comical.

Now I want to tell you about the Monroe doctrine. We think very nicely we think very well of the Monroe doctrine.

American painter painting in French country near railroad track. Mobilisation locomotive passes with notification for villages.

Where are American tourists to buy my pictures sacre nom d'un pipe says the american painter.

American painter sits in cafe and contemplates empty pocket book as taxi cabs file through Paris carrying French soldiers to the battle of the Marne. I guess I'll be a taxi driver here in gay Paree says the american painter.

Painter sits in studio trying to learn names of streets with help of Bretonne peasant femme de menage. He becomes taxi driver. Ordinary street scene in war time Paris.

Being lazy about getting up in the mornings he spends some of his dark nights in teaching Bretonne femme de menage peasant girl how to drive the taxi so she can replace him when he wants to sleep.

America comes into the war american painter wants to be american soldier. Personnel officer interviews him. What have you been doing, taxiing. You know Paris, Secret Service for you go on taxiing.

He goes on taxiing and he teaches Bretonne f. m. english so she can take his place if need be.

One night he reads his paper under the light. Policeman tells him to move up, don't want to wants to read.

Man comes up wants to go to the station.

Painter has to take him. Gets back, reading again.

Another man comes wants to go to the station. Painter takes him.

Comes back to read again. Two american officers come up.

Want to go to the station.

Painter says Tired of the station take you to Berlin if you like. No station.

Officers say give you a lot of you take us outside town on way to the south, first big town.

He says alright got to stop at home first to get his coat.

Stops at home calls out to Bretonne f. m. Get busy telegraph to your relations, you have them all over, ask have you any american officers staying forever. Be back to-morrow.

Back to-morrow. Called up by chief secret service. Goes to see him. Money has been disappearing out of quartermaster's department in chunks. You've got a free hand. Find out something.

Goes home. Finds f. m. Bretonne surrounded with telegrams and letters from relatives. Americans everywhere but everywhere. She groans. Funny Americans everywhere but everywhere they all said. Many funny Americans everywhere. Two Americans not so funny here my fifth cousin says, she is helping in the hospital in Avignon. Such a sweet american soldier. So young so tall so tender. Not very badly hurt but will stay a long long time. He has been visited by american officers who live in a villa. Two such nice ladies live there too and they spend and they spend, they buy all the good sweet food in Avignon. "Is that something William Sir," says the Bretonne f. m.

Its snowing but no matter we will get there in the taxi. Take us two days and two nights you inside and me out. Hurry. They start, the funny little taxi goes over the mountains with and without assistance, all tired out he is inside, she driving when they turn down the hill into Avignon. Just then two Americans on motor cycles come on and Bretonne f. m. losing her head grand smash. American painter wakes up burned, he sees the two and says by God and makes believe he is dead. The two are very helpful. A team comes along and takes american painter and all to hospital. Two Americans ride off on motor cycles direction of Nimes and Pont du Gard.

Arrival at hospital, interview with the wounded Americans who described two american officers who had been like brothers to him, didn't think any officers could be so chummy with a soldier. Took me out treated me, cigarettes everything fine.

Where have they gone on to, to Nimes.

Yes Pont du Gard.

70

American painter in bed in charge of french nursing nun but manages to escape and leave for Pont du Gard in mended taxi. There under the shadow of that imperishable monument of the might and industry of ancient Rome exciting duel. French gendarme american painter, taxi, f. m. Bretonne, two american crooks with motor cycles on which they try to escape over the top of the Pont du Gard, great stunt, they are finally captured. They have been the receivers of the stolen money.

After many other adventures so famous has become the american painter, Bretonne femme de menage and taxi that in the march under the arch at the final triumph of the allies the taxi at the special request of General Pershing brings up the rear of the procession after the tanks, the Bretonne driving and the american painter inside waving the american flag Old Glory and the tricolor

CURTAIN.

Nature and the Emotions

*Gertrude Stein's first literary decade brought her closer
and closer to the expression of what Donald Sutherland (p.
65) has called "the continuous presence of active mind applied to something alive." Her second literary decade moved
towards the increasingly accurate description of an inner
and outer reality—a reality perceived in the moment and in
flux, meaning nothing, as James (Kallen, p. 76) wrote,
"but what it immediately is."*

*During these two decades she had broken away from many
literary conventions. Narrative was the first to go. The language of logic was another. Discursive writing was a third.
Traditional punctuation a fourth. Meaning, in the Aristotelian
sense, a fifth. Traditional literary forms a sixth. There were
others.*

*In their place, Gertrude Stein found other, mutually con-
sistent expressive means: the narrative of the moment, the
description of perceptual flux; the substituting of "a con-
ceptual order for the perceptual order in which . . . experience
originally comes," as James (Kallen, p. 77) worded it, to
create compositions; direct writing instead of "writing
about"; sentences and paragraphs which stood on their own
feet, without the need for internal punctuation to help the
reader; ultimate meaning instead of meaning beyond the
words themselves; the "portrait" and the non-dramatic play
as literary genres.*

*All this required vigorous literary thinking and broke new
ground in her time. It required an intellectual exercise of*

73

great concentration and brought very little public recognition or reward or understanding to Gertrude Stein.

The next two decades of her writing were equally explora-tory and equally filled with novel applications of her core theories.

It may come as a surprise that Gertrude Stein, after all this intellectual endeavor, had her "Romantic Period". As an ex-tension of her desire to "use everything", she now included nature and the emotions in her compositions.

The major works of this period are the "landscape" plays, a considerable body of "domestic poetry", An Acquaintance with Description *(1926), the opera* Four Saints in Three Acts *(1927), and the novel* Lucy Church Amiably *(1927).*

The work abounds in references to rural life: plants, vege-tables, fruits, blooming flowers, waterfalls, animals—the "beauties of nature hills valleys trees fields and birds." The "Advertisement" for Lucy Church Amiably *adequately exemplifies the prose style.*

At the same time, Gertrude Stein developed the idea of the play as landscape—that is, "like a movement in and out with which anybody looking on can keep in time (Lectures In America, p. *131).* Operas and Plays *(1932) contains many of these. "A Saint in Seven" (1922) is an excellent example, full of movement and landscape as "absolute presence".*

ADVERTISEMENT

Lucy Church Amiably. There is a church and it is in Lucey and it has a steeple and the steeple is a pagoda and there is no reason for it and it looks like something else. Beside this there is amiably and this comes from the paragraph.

Select your song she said and it was done and then she said and it was done with a nod and then she bent her head in the direction of the falling water. Amiably.

This altogether makes a return to romantic nature that is it makes a landscape look like an engraving in which there are some people, after all if they are to be seen there they feel as pretty as they look and this makes it have a river a gorge an inundation and a remarkable meadowed mass which is whatever they use not to feed but to bed cows. Lucy Church Amiably is a novel of romantic beauty and nature and of Lucy Church and John Mary and Simon Therese.

A SAINT IN SEVEN

I thought perhaps that we would win by human means, I knew we could win if we did win but I did not think that we could win by human means, and now we have won by human means.

A saint followed and not surrounded.

LIST OF PERSONAGES

1. A saint with a lily.

Second. A girl with a rooster in front of her and a bush of strange flowers at her side and a small tree behind her.

3. A guardian of a museum holding a cane.

4. A woman leaning forward.

5. A woman with a sheep in front of her a small tree behind her.

75

6. A woman with black hair and two bundles one under each arm.

7. A night watchman of a hotel who does not fail to stand all the time.

8. A very stout girl with a basket and flowers summer flowers and the flowers are in front of a small tree.

SAINTS IN SEASON

See Saints in seven.

And how do royalists accuse themselves.

Saints.

Saint Joseph.

In pleading sadness length of sadness in pleading length of sadness and no sorrow. No sorrow and no sadness length of sadness.

A girl addresses a bountiful supply of seed to feed a chicken. Address a bountiful supply of trees to shade them. Address a bountiful supply to them.

A guardian.

In days and nights beside days are followed by daisies. We find them and they find them and water finds them and they grow best where we meant to suggest. We suggested that we would go there again. A woman leaning forward.

She was necessarily taken to be no taller.

A girl.

If she may say what she will say she will say that there were a quantity of voices and they were white and then darker.

A woman with two bundles.

If she did it to be useful if she did not even attract the same throne. What did I say. Did royalists say that they did not have this to say to-day.

Standing.

Measure an alarm by refusing to alarm them and they this not as a disaster but as a pretension. Do you pretend to be unfavorable to their thought.

Eighth.

If you hold heavily heavily instead. Instead of in there. Did you not intend to show this to them.

Saint.

A Saint.

76

Saint and very well I thank you.
Two in bed.
Two in bed.
Yes two in bed.
They had eaten.
Two in bed.
They had eaten.
Two in bed.
She says weaken
If she said.
She said two in bed.
She said they had eaten.
She said yes two in bed.
She said weaken.

Do not acknowledge to me that seven are said that a Saint and seven that it is said that a saint in seven that there is said to be a saint in seven.

Now as to illuminations.

They are going to illuminate and every one is to put into their windows their most beautiful object and every one will say and the streets will be crowded everyone will say look at it. They do say look at it.

To look at it. They will look at it. They will say look at it.

If it should rain they will all be there. If it should be windy they will all be there. Who will be there. They will all be there.

Names of streets named after the saint. Names of places named after the saint. Names of saints named after the saint. Names of sevens named after the saint. The saints in sevens.

Noon-light for Roman arches.

He left fairly early.

Let them make this seen.

Louise giggled.

Michael was not angry nor was he stuttering nor was he able to silence them. He was angry he was stuttering and he was able to answer them.

They were nervous.

Josephine was able to be stouter. Amelia was really not repaid.

And the taller younger and weaker older and straighter one said come to eat again.

Michael was not able to come angrily to them. He angrily muttered for them.

Louise was separated to Heloise and not by us. So then you see saints for them.

Louise.

Heloise.

Amelia.

Josephine.

Michael and Elinor.

Seven, a saint in seven and in this way it was not Paul. Paul was deprived of nothing. Saint in seven a saint in seven.

Who.

A saint in seven.

Owls and bees.

If you please.

Paul makes honey and orange trees.

Michael makes coal and celery.

Louise makes rugs and reasonably long.

Heloise makes the sea and she settles well away from it.

Amelia does not necessarily please. She does not place herself near linen.

Josephine measures a little toy and she may be no neater.

Eleanor has been more satisfied and feeble. She does not look as able to stay nor does she seem as able to go any way.

Saints in seven makes italics sombre.

I make fun of him of her.

I make fun of them.

They make fun of them of this. They make fun of him of her.

She makes fun of of them of him.

He makes fun of them of her.

They make fun of her.

He makes fun of them.

She makes fun of him.

I make fun of them.

We have made them march. She has made a procession.

A saint in seven and there were six. A saint in seven and there were eight. A saint in seven.

If you know who pleads who precedes who succeeds.

He leads.

He leads and they follow. One two three four and as yet there are no more.

A saint in seven.

And when do they sleep again. A ring around the moon is seen to follow the moon and the moon is in the center of the ring and the ring follows the moon.

Sleeping, to-day sleeping to-day is nearly a necessity and to-day coals reward the five. One two three four five. Corals reward the five. In this way they are not leaning with the intention of being a hindrance to satisfaction.

A saint in seven is told of bliss.

I will know why they open so.

Carefully seen to be safely arranged.

One two three four five six seven. A saint in seven.

To begin in this way.

Carefully attended carefully attended to this.

If we had seen if they had seen if we had seen what was in between, they went very slowly so that we might know but to be slow and we were not slow and to show and they showed it and we did not decide because we had already come to a decision.

Saints in seven are a very large number: Seven and seven is not as pretty as five and five. And five and five need not mean more. Now to remember how to mean to be gay. Gayly the boxer the boxer very gayly depresses no one. He seems he does seem he dreams he does dream he seems to dream.

Extra readiness to recall himself to these places. Thanks so much for startling. Do not by any means start to worship in order to be excellent. He is excellent again and again.

A saint can share expenses he can share and he can be interested in their place. Their place is plentifully sprinkled as they bend forward. And no one does mean to contend any more.

A saint in seven plentifully.

None of it is good.

It has been said that the woods are the poor man's overcoat but we have found the mountains which are near by and not high can be an overcoat to us. Can he be an overcoat to us.

A saint in seven wished to be convinced by us that the mountains near by and not high can give protection from the wind. One does not have to consider rain because it cannot rain here. A saint in seven wishes to be convinced by us that the mountains which are near by would act as a protection to those who find it cold and yet when one considers that nothing is suffering neither men women children lambs roses and broom, broom is yellow when one considers that neither broom, roses lambs men children and women none of them suffer neither here nor in the mountains near by the mountains are not high and if it were not true that every one had to be sure that they were there every one would be persuaded that they had persuaded that they had been persuaded that this was true.

He told us that he knew that the name was the same. A saint in seven can declare this to be true.

He comes again. Yes he comes again and what does he say he says do you know this do you refuse no more than you give. That is the way to spell it do you refuse no more than you give.

He searches for more than one word. He manages to eat finally and as he does so and as he does so and as he does so he manages to cut the water in two. If water is flowing down a canal and it is understood that the canal is full if the canal has many outlets for irrigation purposes and the whole country is irrigated if even the mountains are irrigated by the canal and in this way neither oil nor seeds nor wood is needed and it is needed by them why then do the examples remain here examples of industry of cowardice of pleasure of reasonable sight seeing of objections and of lands and oceans. We do not know oceans. We do not know measures. Measure and measure and then decide that a servant beside, what is a servant beside. No one knows how easily he can authorise him to go, how easily she can authorise her to go how easily they can authorise them to come and to go. I authorise you to come and go. I authorise you to go. I authorise you to go and come.

Literary Music

The whole resonance of romantic nature and the amplitude of bucolic emotions which Gertrude Stein rendered in the "Romantic Period" now underwent a concentration and refinement. Numerous short works consolidate the efforts of the "Spanish Period" and the "Romantic (or San Remy) Period" into a flexible, melodious style of variety and charm, unified by the great authority of the writer's voice as she now makes a kind of literary chamber music:

"I concentrated the internal melody of existence that I had learned in relation to things seen into the feeling I then had there in San Remy of light and air moving and being still." (Lectures In America, p. 19).

"A Valentine to Sherwood Anderson" (1922) exemplifies this period, its increasing focus and gentle playfulness.

A VALENTINE TO SHERWOOD ANDERSON

IDEM THE SAME

I knew too that through them I knew too that he was through, I knew too that he threw them. I knew too that they were through, I knew too I knew too, I knew I knew them.

I knew to them.

If they tear a hunter through, if they tear through a hunter, if they tear through a hunt and a hunter, if they tear through the different sizes of the six, the different sizes of the six which are these, a woman with a white package under one arm and a black package under the other arm and dressed in brown with a white blouse, the second Saint Joseph the third a hunter in a blue coat and black garters and a plaid cap, a fourth a knife grinder who is full faced and a very little woman with black hair and a yellow hat and an excellently smiling appropriate soldier. All these as you please.

In the meantime examples of the same lily. In this way please have you rung.

WHAT DO I SEE.

A very little snail.
A medium sized turkey.
A small band of sheep.
A fair orange tree.
All nice wives are like that.
Listen to them from here.
Oh.
You did not have an answer.
Here.
Yes.

A VERY VALENTINE.

Very fine is my valentine.
Very fine and very mine.
Very mine is my valentine very mine and very fine.
Very fine is my valentine and mine, very fine very mine and
mine is my valentine.

WHY DO YOU FEEL DIFFERENTLY

Why do you feel differently about a very little snail and a big
one.
Why do you feel differently about a medium sized turkey and a
very large one.
Why do you feel differently about a small band of sheep and
several sheep that are riding.
Why do you feel differently about a fair orange tree and one
that has blossoms as well.
Oh very well.
All nice wives are like that.
To Be.
No Please.
To Be.
They can please
Not to be
Do they please.
Not to be
Do they not please
Yes please.
Do they please
No please.
Do they not please
No please.
Do they please.
Please.

84

If you please.
And if you please.
And if they please
And they please.
To be pleased.
Not to be pleased.
Not to be displeased.
To be pleased and to please.

KNEELING

One two three four five six seven eight nine and ten.
The tenth is a little one kneeling and giving away a rooster with
this feeling.
I have mentioned one, four five seven eight and nine.
Two is also giving away an animal.
Three is changed as to disposition.
Six is in question if we mean mother and daughter, black and
black caught her, and she offers to be three she offers it to me.
That is very right and should come out below and just so.

BUNDLES FOR THEM.

A History Of Giving Bundles.

We were able to notice that each one in a way carried a bundle,
they were not a trouble to them nor were they all bundles as some
of them were chickens some of them pheasants some of them sheep
and some of them bundles, they were not a trouble to them and
then indeed we learned that it was the principal recreation and

they were so arranged that they were not given away, and to-day they were given away.

I will not look at them again.

They will not look for them again.

They have not seen them here again.

They are in there and we hear them again.

In which way are stars brighter than they are. When we have come to this decision. We mention many thousands of buds. And when I close my eyes I see them.

If you hear her snore

It is not before you love her

You love her so that to be her beau is very lovely

She is sweetly there and her curly hair is very lovely

She is sweetly here and I am very near and that is very lovely.

She is my tender sweet and her little feet are stretched out well which is a treat and very lovely

Her little tender nose is between her little eyes which close and are very lovely.

She is very lovely and mine which is very lovely.

ON HER WAY.

If you can see why she feels that she kneels if you can see why he knows that he shows what he bestows, if you can see why they share what they share, need we question that there is no doubt that by this time if they had intended to come they would have sent some notice of such intention. She and they and indeed the decision itself is not early dissatisfaction.

IN THIS WAY.

Keys please, it is useless to alarm any one it is useless to alarm some one it is useless to be alarming and to get fertility in gardens in salads in heliotrope and in dishes. Dishes and wishes are mentioned and dishes and wishes are not capable of darkness. We like sheep. We like sheep. And so does he.

LET US DESCRIBE.

Let us describe how they went. It was a very windy night and the road although in excellent condition and extremely well graded has many turnings and although the curves are not sharp the rise is considerable. It was a very windy night and some of the larger vehicles found it more prudent not to venture. In consequence some of those who had planned to go were unable to do so. Many others did go and there was a sacrifice, of what shall we, a sheep, a hen, a cock, a village, a ruin, and all that and then that having been blessed let us bless it.

Syntax and Elucidation (1923 ff.)

" . . . *now I am trying grammar and eliminating sight and sound*," *Gertrude Stein wrote the editor of* transition *magazine in 1923.*

The problem of syntax had been with her ever since her first decision to shift out of the narrative past tense into the "participial style" of The Making of Americans.

This preoccupation with the formal and informal properties of language and the ways words may be patterned into sentences was intensified, however, after 1922, and accounts for much of her writing and its character up to the 1930's. The key work is How To Write *(1931).*

A second, and steadily increasing preoccupation of this decade was how to elucidate for herself and for others the nature and meaning of her work. "An Elucidation" (1923) was a first attempt, but completely non-audience oriented. Composition as Explanation *(1926), the Oxford-Cambridge lecture, was the first public attempt. Another was "Genuine Creative Ability" (1930), written for her friend, Henry McBride, editor of* Creative Art.

"An Elucidation" is, of course direct elucidation. All of Gertrude Stein's syntactical games are played at once in this explanation by direct example.

"Genuine Creative Ability", an elucidation in the form of a letter, again makes no concessions to the reader who is looking for a traditional "explanation". Gertrude Stein's

89

mind, as always, is composing. She demonstrates genuine creative ability in the moment, "and winds up", as Donald Sutherland puts it (p. 91), "with a result that exists in and for itself."

AN ELUCIDATION

Halve Rivers and Harbours.

Elucidation.
First as Explanation.
Elucidate the problem of halve.
Halve and have.
Halve Rivers and Harbours.
Have rivers and harbours.
You do see that halve rivers and harbours, halve rivers and harbours, you do see that halve rivers and harbours makes halve rivers and harbours and you do see, you do see that you that you do not have rivers and harbours when you halve rivers and harbours, you do see that you can halve rivers and harbours.
I refuse have rivers and harbours I have refused. I do refuse have rivers and harbours. I receive halve rivers and harbours, I accept halve rivers and harbours.
I have elucidated the pretence of halve rivers and harbours and the acceptation of halve rivers and harbours.
This is a new preparation.
Do not share.
He will not bestow.
They can meditate.
I am going to do so.
I have an explanation of this in this way. If we say, Do not share, he will not bestow they can meditate I am going to do so, we have organised an irregular commonplace and we have made excess return to rambling. I always like the use of these, but not particularly.

Madrigal and Mardigras.

I do not deny these except in regard to one thing they remind me of Em which is a name for Emma. I have always been fond of writing the letter M, and so although Mardigras and Madrigal have more appreciation from me than they might they do not make

91

more questions and more answers passing. He was as if he were going to pass an examination.

I will now give more examples.

She is in and out

It is placed in there

Happily say so

Too happily say so

Very communicative.

I will give other examples to you. I will give the same example to you and to you.

Place. In a place

A place for everything and everything in its place.

In place in place of everything, in a place.

Again search for me.

She looked for me at me.

May we seat.

May we be having a seat.

May we be seated

May I see

May I see

Martha

May I see Martha.

May I see.

May I see.

I have written the best examples of all before

Able

Idle.

There are four words in all.

There

Why

There

Why

There

Able

Idle.

There are seven in all.

A stall for each.

As tall as each one.

As there are all and four and seven, and seven and four and are four in all and a stall for each one.

We do not think at all of a stall as a box, there used to be a box a loose box and now there are no loose boxes. Boxes are arranged with cement, and so our fancy pleases, and so we may fancy as we please, we may fancy what we please.

There is an excellent example and now I will explain away as if I have been sitting for my portrait every day.

In this way I have made every one understand arithmetic.

To begin elucidating.

If I say I stand and pray.

If I say I stand and I stand and you understand and if I say I pray I pray to-day if you understand me to say I pray to-day you understand prayers and portraits.

You understand portraits and prayers.

You understand.

You do understand.

An introduction and an explanation and I completely introduce as you please.

I completely introduce. Yes you do.

Yes you do.

Yes you do is the longest example and will come at the end.

The longest example.

Yes you do.

Will come at the end.

Disturb.

Seated here

I know how to please her.

If I know

If you know how to throw how to throw or to go. I feel that you easily understand that preparation is not everything I understand everything. And now to explain where preparation and preparing show this as an expedition. An expedition is a journey to and for.

Dealing in accelerated authority.

Do not notice this.

Dealing in their delight or daylight.

Do not notice this properly.

Dealing in a regularly arranged decision.

When you wish to diminish.

Let me explain properly.

Properly speaking there is no fear that he will not be prayed for out loud.

Properly speaking there is no fear of neglect. And all words furnish here. I have a great many examples very often.

We do very often.

An explanation of not at all.

Not at all very nearly furnishes us with an illustration. We have mainly added to that.

Now to seriously mean seldom.

It is only seldom that we are selected.

And she knows me.

I will now explain dishes.

I have explained that.

I never do see that I never do see you do see me

You do see me. A serious explanation.

To explain means to give a reason for in order. He adores her.

You must not be excited before and after. You must make a choice.

I thought perhaps he would not make a choice.

Before and after.

This is an example a very good example or an example.

This is an example or a very good example.

Let me lead you to find this. If in beginning you mention explaining, could he be angry could he really be angry that you had not explained it to him.

Suppose or supposing that you had an invitation, suppose some one had been very inviting supposing some one had given him an invitation supposing you had been inviting him to listen to an explanation suppose there had been an explanation supposing you had given an explanation, I can explain visiting. I can explain how it happened accidentally that fortunately no explanation was necessary.

I explain wording and painting and sealing and closing. I explain opening and reasoning and rolling, I was just rolling. What did he say. He said I was not mistaken and yet I had not when he was not prepared for an explanation I had not begun explaining. It is in a way a cause for congratulation. It is in a way cause for congratulation.

And now to seriously discuss my needing and to discuss very seriously why they have asked for my mediation.

To begin now.

Small examples are preferable.

They are preferred.
And do they stop them. And yet do they stop them.
Preferred as to preference I prefer them.
If you connect them do you connect them.
In this way.
If small examples are preferable and are preferred and they are connected in this way we may say yesterday was nearly seventeen days earlier than to-day, seventeen days earlier in any way. It is connected in this way. Small examples are preferable. They are preferred.

An instance

Tremble for small examples. I hope you received the three volumes safely.
Tremble for small examples.
It is not easy.
A third part is added to the top and bottom and the middle part is added in between.
Some examples simply
I tire more quickly than you do.
Some examples simply.
Small examples are preferable.
Small examples are preferred.
Brown and white. The nigger and the night and mistaken for mean. I didn't mean to.
I do read better there.
Come on
He consolidated it. That you must not do.

Elucidation.

The sad procession of the unkilled bull. And they stand around.
Two next.
To be next to it.
To be annexed.
To be annexed to it.
We understand that you undertake to overthrow our undertaking.
This is not originally said to frame words this is originally said to underestimate words.
Do you believe in stretches, stretches of time stretches of scenery and stretches of thirds.
Every third time we rhyme, in this way influence is general. Let me recognise copies.
Extra gum.
Gum extra.
Extra gum.
An extra gum.
An extra rubber.
An extra oil.
An extra soap.
And an extra wish.
Wish and White.
Reasons are right.
White and wish.
Reasons for which they have most occasion. They have more occasion for one wish than for another wish.
Do you all understand if you please.
Do you all understand why I explain.
Do you all understand elucidation and extra addresses.
Do you all understand why she sees me.
Do you all understand practice and precept.
Do you all understand principal and secondary.
Do you all understand extraneous memory.
Let me see how earnestly you plead for me.
Let me see.

More beginning.

I begin you begin we begin they begin. They began we began you began I began.

I began you begin we begin they begin. They begin you begin we begin I began.

You began and I began.

I feel the need of a walk in ceremony, of a talk in ceremony of chalk in ceremony. I feel the need of chalk in ceremony.

And it was used too, it was used too.

A settled explanation.

I know the difference between white marble and black marble. White and black marble make a checker board and I never mention either.

Either of them you know very well that I may have said no.

Now to explain.

Did I say explanations mean across and across and carry. Carry me across.

Another explanation.

I think I won't
I think I will
I think I will
I think I won't
I think I won't
I think I will

I think I will
I think I won't.
I think I won't
I think I will
I think I will
I think I won't
I think I will
I think I won't
I think I will
I think I won't.
I think I will
I think I won't
I think I won't
I think I won't
I think I won't
I think I will
I think I won't
Of course
I think I will
I think I won't
I think I won't
I think I will
This is a good example if you do not abuse it.
Where they like.
Can follow where they like.
I think this is a good example.
I think I will.
I am afraid I have been too careful.
I think I will.
Two examples and then an elucidation and a separation of one example from the other one.
I think I will.
Then very certainly we need not repeat.
Can there at this rate can there have been at this rate more and more.
Can at this rate can there have been at this rate can there have been more and more at this rate.
At this rate there can not have been there can not have been at this rate there can not have been more and more at this rate. At this rate there can not have been more and more. There can not have

been at this rate, there can not have been more and more at this rate there can not have been more and more at this rate.

What did I say. Full of charms I said.

Full of what. Full of charms I said.

What did I say, full of charms I said.

If in order to see incidentally incidentally I request to see extraordinarily.

If in order to see incidentally I request to see.

I see you I see you too.

A Question.

Should you see me too.

Not a question.

Now to combine all this together to make more.

I stopped, I stopped myself.

Combine all these together to make more.

Elucidation.

If in beginning, if in a beginning, I begin to be connectedly and carefully and collectedly if I agree, if in beginning I agree, then I agree you agree and we agree.

If he can recall a boast of victory, I can refuse to be resolutely sure of what he and I both mean to collect.

Now do you see that this is a thing to erase and eradicate.

Do you not see it clearly.

Let me refuse to repair it.

He said that repairs are excellently made.

We have combined to be not at all principally paid. Paid and paid. Do you see halve rivers and harbours and there is no connection.

An example of an event.

If it is an event just by itself is there a question.

Tulips is there a question.

Pets is there a question.

Furs is there a question.

Folds is there a question.

Is there anything in question.

To begin to be told that after she had seen and said she wrote and read.

She read it and she said, she said it and she read it, she wrote and she did indeed change her residence. I have been told that this is an event. If it is an event just by itself if there a question. A great many climates have been quoted. In this way we may expect to see that they have this to see to too. May we quote again.

Should you see me too.

All events. Carrie all events.

All events carry.

In this way researchers are easily read.

A short example of stretches of variety.

She made white flowers resemble lilies of the valley and she said do not mean to be prepared to have a goddess of plenty stand in front of a picture.

In this way you see that I have not succeeded.

If at first you do not succeed try try again.

She found china easily adaptable. In use the word china she had in mind porcelain and also painted wood and even painted tin and dishes. She sometimes felt the need of silver and radishes.

Do you measure this by this measure. And altogether what did you say you were to elucidate to-day. By this I mean for this to be seen.

You know how we make it do so and more so, how we make it more so, how we make it even more so.

I lead up to a description of all the birds.

The birds have meant to interest me so have the horses and so indeed have the preparations for cows. So indeed have the preparations so indeed have the preparations, so indeed.

I can see and you can see, you can see and so can I see that I have not made more of it than needs to be made of it. In every way you are satisfied and we have given satisfaction and we have not meant to be swamped by other considerations. And again and once

100

more and frequently from time to time no one has suffered in any way and we are satisfied. It may even be said as if in a joke those who might have to be considered are satisfied. Can you kindly smile.

And now we add that which makes a whole history plainer. What did I say. I said he would tell me the complete history of his life and times. And in this way we recollect perfectly just when he was prepared and just when he was prepared.

Suppose for instance suppose as an instance we mention success. I succeed and you succeed. Yes you succeed very well. You do succeed very well. You do succeed very very well.

Five examples and then the long example entitled Yes you do.

First Example

How pleasantly I feel contented with that. Contented with the example, content with the example.

As if one example was meant to be succeeded by an example. I remember that he said they can prepare to have it here and to have it there to have it here and there. We have said there to have it there.

First Example

Suppose, to suppose, suppose a rose is a rose is a rose is a rose.

To suppose, we suppose that there arose here and there that here and there there arose an instance of knowing that there are here and there that there are there that they will prepare, that they do care to come again. Are they to come again.

In this way I have explained that to them and for them that for them alone that to them alone that to them and for them we have no depression. The law covers this, if you say made of fruit or if you say made by the aid of or made with the aid of fruit, or made by using fruit or made with fruit, for the fruit, you see how suddenly if there is in question if there can be any question, what would then compare with their description, with the description of this description. I describe all the time.

The second example is an example of action.

What action.

If you arrange the door, if you arrange the door and the floor. I have lost most of my interest in politics, still it is more interesting than the theatre. Brenner says that.

In action.

In every action we can take he knows that if the hair is there and the ears hear and the Causars share and they linger and if they linger and finger if they finger their pair, if they finger the pair and care to be more hesitant than before if they are to partake in this action, the action is memorable. They can be declared coloured by their wish. Wish how can we who are Americans and not credulous remember that there has been written the wished on wish. Do you smile if you do you please you applaud me you say action to take action to behave in action to see their action to dominate their action and their action and do you expect what has been said that some are attempting to hit some one hit some one who was not the one intended to be hit and this is not common this is not common this does not commonly happen in action in their action.

Example third is the one that will show how often every one has cause abundant cause for this and for that.

To explain I will explain. To take the place to take the place of this. In that way. Please help to avail yourself will you please avail yourself of your opportunities.

In this way and in that way they may or they may not, they may avail themselves of their opportunities. We had a long conversation about the way they may and they may not about the way they may avail themselves of their opportunities.

Let us imagine that every one is interested in my wife and children.

One and a million. A million or three. There are three there and here and there there are a hundred and three here and here and there there they are.

How do you do.

We know why we compare we compare this to that, and we share we can share we do share what do they share what do they happen to do what do they to do, what do they do, what do they happen to do why do they do they do it, why do they not do it, why they do they not do this. Do it, oh do do it. Do you do it. How do you do, how do you do it, how do you do it in this way in that way, in the way. They are not in the way. We say they are not there and they say they are here and we say they are here and there. Continue to expect me. I do expect you. You do expect me. We do expect you. We do. We do expect to have you we do expect, do you expect, do you, do you how do you do, how do you do this, how do I do this, how do I do it, how do I do it. How do I do it, I do it, you do it, yes I do do it.

A third example can be too long.

A fourth example shows more plainly what it does show, what does it show, I see you and you see me, I see that you see and you see that I see. A fourth example shows a tendency to declaration.

I declare that they say from Tuesday till Saturday and Friday afternoon too.

I declare I do declare.

And he when we see that they are not as we understood they would be when we see, when we say we see we hear, and when we say we hear we feel and when we say we feel we see and when we say we see we hear.

In this we declare we declare all of us declare what do you declare, declare to me. Declarations rapidly reunited. Action and reaction are equal and opposite. Astonishment means list of persons and places and if she were to be represented there if she were to be represented there. Call me a smiler and fit the fifth exactly.

I fit the fifth exactly.

Yes you do.

This is not an instance. Fit the fifth exactly. Exactly fit the fifth fit it for the fifth. The fifth in this way makes rounding out rounder. If it is round around and rounder if it is around and we tell all we know let me explain directly and indirectly. In the fifth instance there was no coincidence.

Every night generally.

I lead to Yes you do. You lead to yes you do, we lead to yes you do they lead to yes you do.

Yes you do otherwise understood. Otherwise understood. Yes you do. We understand you undertake to overthrow our undertaking. We understand you do understand that we will understand it correctly. Correctly and incorrectly, prepare and prepared, patiently and to prepare, to be prepared and to be particularly not particularly prepared. Do prepare to say Portraits and Prayers, do prepare to say that you have prepared portraits and prayers and that you prepare and that I prepare.

Yes you do.
Organisers.
Yes you do.
Organisation.
Yes you do and you, you do.
To portraits and to prayers.
Yes you do.

GENUINE CREATIVE ABILITY

Could I say no to you never. *Creative Art* reminds me that the Guggenheim prize is always to be given for genuine creative ability and the scheme of study is always sent along confidentially. Now what is genuine creative ability. We know. And we have not sent it along confidentially. Here it is. There are several subjects about which I can write. First Basket, then paragraphs, then Tonney, then three and I am through with three. And then me.

I have just changed my mind. I have just had that experience. Listen to me.

He looks like a young man grown old. That is a sentence that they could use.

I was overcome with remorse. It was my fault that my wife did not have a cow. This sentence they cannot use.

Now listen to me.

I have had a very curious experience.

If they had been one after the other it makes no difference, first I saw one well first I saw one. His name I will not mention. I was

pleased, very flattered to be pleased. If it was not difficult it was
not closed. I do not deny that I love to have them one at a time. But
if they are not one at a time then I see them all the time. It finally
came about that all three of them were of no particular use. I will
not mention names because nobody will have to think at all anyway. That is the end of that.

After that in a way before that one might have it in between
about that. Tonney. I will mention him because I like to. It would
be a pleasure. He used to think that it would be a pleasure. He
used not to think. That it would be a pleasure. And now without it
at all it is a pleasure. That is Tonney he was made for Tonney
Kristian and now he is Kristian Tonney.

Now for the other subjects. Basket. How can you make a dog
obedient.

Tapestry. If tapestry gets crooked it makes no difference it can
be drawn straight.

Paragraphs. How to write. Paragraphs are natural and sentences
are not and if I must forget the reason why.

Thanks very much I am always grateful.

Gertrude Stein.

Postscript. I am very busy finding out what people mean by what
they say. I used to be interested in what they were I am now interested in what they say.   G.S.

Disembodied Movement

Gertrude Stein had explored several aspects of movement —the constant flux William James called "the present moment," the everlasting "coming of concrete novelty into being" she called "the prolonged present", the internal movement of ideas, and the movement of things seen and heard. Particularly in plays she explored the movement of relationships and movement in and out of a landscape setting.

Sometime in the 1930's she conceived the idea of creating entities so vital "that there was something completely contained within itself and being contained within itself was moving, not moving in relation to any thing not moving in relation to itself but just moving." (Lectures In America, p. 202)

This is a complex notion which may perhaps be better understood if we think of such closed systems as the human organism, carrying its own life within itself, or the airborne plane or motorcar carrying within themselves the sources of energy which allow them to achieve great bursts of speed and detachment from the parent environment.

The degree to which Gertrude Stein accomplished this sense of detached movement and vitality, even to her own satisfaction, I do not know. Donald Sutherland recognized her "effort to conceive and express sheer happening so intensely that it becomes a thing in itself, that it has final being" (Sutherland, p. 151) as a peak point in her literary career.

The "Portrait of George Hugnet" (1928) Stein considered an example of this phase of her work. She compared it to folding a boat out of paper or putting an apple in a dumpling. It was a kind of union of styles to create a new style. She maintained an interest in this manner through the early 40's, when she wrote "To Bobchen" (1941) a portrait so balanced within itself that it hums and vibrates like a spinning top.

GEORGE HUGNET

George and Genevieve.

Geronimo with a with whether they thought they were with whether.

Without their finding it out. Without. Their finding it out. With whether.

George whether they were about. With their finding their whether it finding it out whether with their finding about it out.

George with their finding it with out.

George whether their with their it whether.

Redoubt out with about.

With out whether it their whether with out doubt.

Azure can with out about.

It is welcome welcome thing.

George in are ring.

Lain away awake.

George in our ring.

George Genevieve Geronimo straightened it out without their finding it out.

Grammar makes George in our ring which Grammar make George in our ring.

Grammar is as disappointed not is as grammar is as disappointed.

Grammar is not as Grammar is as disappointed.

George is in our ring. Grammar is not is disappointed. In are ring.

George Genevieve in are ring.

TO BOBCHEN HAAS

A VILLAGE
ARE YOU READY YET NOT YET

He is always ready
Yet not yet
He is always ready
Let him let

Always be all ready
Yet he will get
Everything all ready
Yet and yet

Identity: Audience Writing (1933-1946)

In 1933, with the publication of The Autobiography of Alice B. Toklas *(1932), Gertrude Stein's private life was over. She became widely known, widely printed, and something of a public figure as a public lecturer. What this did to her as a person and as a writer is a matter of record. The function of this section of the Little Anthology is to suggest what it did to her stylistically.*

Two kinds of writing emerged in the last decade of her life. The first was the writing done with a sense of audience. Books and articles which emerged from this are, besides The Autobiography of Alice B. Toklas, Lectures in America *(1934),* Narration *(1935), "What Are Masterpieces" (1935), "How Writing is Written" (1935),* Everybody's Autobiography *(1936), "An American and France" (1936),* Picasso *(1939)* Paris France *(1939),* Wars I Have Seen *(1942), and "To Americans" from* Brewsie and Willie *(1945). Other shorter works which appeared in newspapers and magazines or served as the texts for radio broadcasts also belong to this category.*

Gertrude Stein knew this was her "secondary" writing, and because it earned money for her she said it mixed her up in her relationship to God and Mammon. The fact that it was done with an audience in mind made it "identity" writing.

However, vast segments of the English speaking public who had never read her before now did. And the prose style, though always marked by what Bridgeman calls the "individual sensibility" or "the personal response" of Gertrude

111

Stein, is usually limpidly clear and frequently persuasive and of great interest.

Two examples of the "Identity Style" are "My Debt to Books" (1939) and "To Americans" from Brewsie and Willie *(1945).*

MY DEBT TO BOOKS

You only add books you never subtract or divide them and any book that is printed is a book. It is nice that nobody writes as they talk and that the printed language is different from the spoken otherwise you could not lose yourself in books and of course you do, you completely do. I always do. I always remember all the detail in the book no matter what the book is and therefore it is necessary to begin it at the beginning to lose yourself in it when I read it again just as I had to when I read it first.

So many books have been important to me, it is like the man who said about automobiles when some one asked him is that mark a good one, all automobiles are good, some might go better than others but they all go, and that is the way books are to me, any book that I can read at all is important to me and I can read most of them, each one does something to me, you have to read a lot of books if you are going to read all your life and read at least five or six books a week, you can read them over and over again but even so it does take a good many if you begin when you are very young and you live a reasonably long life.

Gulliver's Travels Robinson Crusoe, I was surprised when I found a copy of the Swiss Family Robinson on the quays the other day and found on reading it that it was not at all the kind of book I had remembered it to be all the detail was there but the past and the future were very different that is one of the delightful things about the quays you see books that you never thought it would be possible to see again and you buy them for three francs and you read through Shakespeare, Lavengro and Romany Rye, Trollope and Edgar Wallace, and everything in between, of course only English I cannot read any foreign language, I cannot lose myself in them, and so they are not books to me unless they are translated into English. But which have I read the most often, of the novelists, Walter Scott and Anthony Trollope, of the playwriters Shakespeare, of the poets Coleridge, Poe and Wordsworth, at least they stick most to my mind, of miscellaneous George Borrow and when I was young Clarissa Harlowe, which I think to be the greatest of all novels, but I read so much it all means so much to me, never less and never more because if perfection is good more perfection is better but it is always perfect, and books are always complete to me completely books and I can always lose myself in practically any of them.

TO AMERICANS

G.I.s and G.I.s and G.I.s and they have made me come all over patriotic. I was always patriotic, I was always in my way a Civil War veteran, but in between, there were other things, but now there are no other things. And I am sure that this particular moment in our history is more important than anything since the Civil War. We are there where we have to have to fight a spiritual pioneer fight or we will go poor as England and other industrial countries have gone poor, and dont think that communism or socialism will save you, you just have to find a new way, you have to find out how you can go ahead without running away with yourselves, you have to learn to produce without exhausting your country's wealth, you have to learn to be individual and not just mass job workers, you have to get courage enough to know what you feel and not just all be yes or no men, but you have to really learn to express complication, go easy and if you cant go easy go as easy as you can. Remember the depression, dont be afraid to look it in the face and find out the reason why, dont be afraid of the reason why, if you dont find out the reason why you'll go poor and my God how I would hate to have my native land go poor. Find out the reason why, look facts in the face, not just what they all say, the leaders, but every darn one of you so that a government by the people for the people shall not perish from the face of the earth, it wont, somebody else will do it if we lie down on the job, but of all things dont stop, find out the reason why of the depression, find it out each and every one of you and then look the facts in the face. We are Americans.

114

Entity: Really Writing

No matter how much of Gertrude Stein's last writing was colored by the sense of audience, she held back one portion of herself for the "pure" writing she had always done, a kind of musica reservata, *a music reserved to the glory of God. These meditations of her last years encompass such major works as* Four in America *(1933),* The Geographical History Of America Or The Relation Of Human Nature To The Human Mind *(1935), perhaps the children's books,* The World is Round *(1938) and the* Gertrude Stein First Reader *(1948),* Ida, a Novel *(1940),* Brewsie and Willie *(1945), many short pieces done between 1932 and 1946, considerable poetry, including "Stanzas in Meditation" (1932) and the various later theatre works published in* Last Operas and Plays *(1949), notably "Dr. Faustus Lights the Lights" (1938) and "The Mother of Us All" (1946).*

Two examples may indicate the very elevated, philosophical character of this last period.

"Identity A Poem" (1935) is an étude related to the Geographical History. *In the form of a play, it poses the problems of entity and identity taking as its springboard the deceitfully simple* Mother Goose *rhyme to create what Thornton Wilder* (The Geographical History of America, p. 10) *has called "a succession of 'metaphysical metaphors'".*

In quite another vein, but written in the vastly elevated philosophical style, is the concluding aria of Susan B. An-

thony from the last opera "The Mother of Us All" (1946). Perhaps Gertrude Stein's last assessment of herself, her life and her creative work, here she makes her final expressive statement about time, God, and ultimate knowing. All this she compresses into the kind of entity she thought of as "really writing."

IDENTITY A POEM

I am I because my little dog knows me. The figure wanders on alone.

The little dog does not appear because if it did then there would be nothing to fear.

It is not known that anybody who is anybody is not alone and if alone then how can the dog be there and if the little dog is not there is it alone. The little dog is not alone because no little dog could be alone. If it were alone it would not be there.

So then the play has to be like this.

The person and the dog are there and the dog is there and the person is there and where oh where is their identity, is the identity there anywhere.

I say two dogs but say a dog and a dog.

The human mind.   The human mind does play.

The human mind.   Plays because it plays.

Human Nature.   Does not play because it does not play again.

It might desire something but it does not play again.

And so to make excitement and not nervousness into a play.

And then to make a play with just the human mind.

Let us try.

To make a play with human nature and not anything of the human mind.

Pivoines smell like magnolias

Dogs smell like dogs

Men smell like men

And gardens smell differently at different seasons of the year.

Try a play again
Every little play helps
Another play.

There is any difference between resting and waiting.

Does a little dog rest.

Does a little dog wait.

What does the human mind do.

What does human nature do.

There is no in between in a play.
A play could just as well only mean two.
Then it could do
It could really have to do.

The dog.	What could it do.
The human mind.	The human mind too.
Human nature.	Human nature does not have it to do.

What can a dog do and with waiting too.
Yes there is when you have not been told when to cry.
Nobody knows what the human mind is when they are drunk.
Everybody who has a grandfather has had a great grandfather and that great grandfather has had a father. This actually is true of a grandmother who was a granddaughter and grandfather had a father.
Any dog too.
Any time anyone who knows how to write can write to any brother.
Not a dog too.
A dog does not write too.

ANOTHER PLAY

But. But is a place where they can cease to distress her.

ANOTHER PLAY

It does not make any difference what happens to anybody if it does not make a difference what happens to them.
This no dog can say.
Not any dog can say not ever when he is at play.
And so dogs and human nature have no identity.
It is extraordinary that when you are acquainted with a whole family you can forget about them.

ANOTHER PLAY

A man coming.
Yes there is a great deal of use in a man coming but will he

118

come at all if he does come will he come here.

How do you like it if he comes and look like that. Not at all later. Well anyway he does come and if he likes it he will come again.

Later when another man comes

He does not come.

Girls coming. There is no use in girls coming.

Well anyway he does come and if he likes it he will come again.

PART IV

The question of identity.

A PLAY.

I am I because my little dog knows me.

Which is he.

No which is he.

Say it with tears, no which is he.

I am I why.

So there.

I am I where.

ACT I SCENE III

I am I because my little dog knows me.

ACT I SCENE

Now this is the way I had played that play.

But not at all not as one is one.

ACT I SCENE I

Which one is there I am I or another one.

Who is one and one or one is one.

I like a play of acting so and so and a dog my dog is any one of not one.

But we in America are not displaced by a dog oh no no not at all not at all at all displaced by a dog.

SCENE I

A dog chokes over a ball because it is a ball that choked any one.

PART I SCENE I

He has forgotten that he has been choked by a ball no not forgotten because this one the same one is not the one that can choke any one.

SCENE I ACT I

I am I because my little dog knows me, but perhaps he does not and if he did I would not be I. Oh no oh no.

ACT I SCENE I

When a dog is young he seems to be a very intelligent one.
But later well later the dog is older.
And so the dog roams around he knows the one he knows but does that make any difference.
A play is exactly like that.
Chorus   There is no left or right without remembering.
And remembering.
They say there is no left and right without remembering.
Chorus   But there is no remembering the human mind.
Tears   There is no chorus in the human mind.
The land is flat from on high and when they wander.
Chorus   Nobody who has a dog forgets him. They may leave him behind. Oh yes they may leave him behind.
Chorus   There is no memory in the human mind.
And the result
May be and the result
If I am I then my little dog knows me.
The dog listens while they prepare food.
Food might be connected by the human mind but it is not.

120

And how do you like what you are
And how are you what you are
And has this to do with the human mind.
Chorus   And has this to do with the human mind.
Chorus   And is human nature not at all interesting. It is not.

I am I because my little dog knows me.
Chorus   That does not prove anything about you it only proves
           something about the dog.
Chorus   Of course nobody can be interested in human nature.
Chorus   Nobody is.
Chorus   Nobody is interested in human nature.
Chorus   Not even a dog
Chorus   It has nothing to do human nature has nothing to do
           with anything.
Chorus   No not with a dog
Tears   No not with a dog.
Chorus   I am I because my little dog knows
Chorus   Yes there I told you human nature is not at all in-
           teresting.

And the human mind.
Chorus   And the human mind
Tears   And the human mind
Chorus   Yes and the human mind.
Of course the human mind
Has that anything to do with I am I because my little dog knows
me.
What is the chorus.
Chorus   What is the chorus.
Anyway there is the question of identity.
What is the use of being a little boy if you are to grow up to be
a man.
Chorus   No the dog is not the chorus.

Any scene may be scene II
Chorus   And act II
No any act can be act one and two.

I am I because my little dog knows me even if the little dog is a big one and yet a little dog knowing me does not really make me be I no not really because after all being I I am I has really nothing to do with the little dog knowing me, he is my audience, but an audience never does prove to you that you are you.
And does a little dog making a noise make the same noise.
He can almost say the b in bow wow.
I have not been mistaken.
Chorus   Some kinds of things not and some kinds of things.

I am I yes sir I am I.
I am I yes madame am I I.
When I am I am I I.
And my little dog is not the same thing as I am I.
Chorus   Oh is it.
With tears in my eyes oh is it.
And there we have the whole thing
Am I I.
And if I am I because my little dog knows me am I I.
Yes sir am I I.
The dog answers without asking because the dog is the answer to anything that is that dog.
But not I.
Without tears but not I.

The necessity of ending is not the necessity of beginning.
Chorus   How finely that is said.

An end of a play is not the end of a day.

122

After giving.

THE MOTHER OF US ALL
(CONCLUDING ARIA)

Susan B.'s voice: We cannot retrace our steps, going forward may be the same as going backwards. We cannot retrace our steps, retrace our steps. All my long life, all my life, we do not retrace our steps, all my long life, but.
(A silence a long silence)
But—we do not retrace our steps, all my long life, and here, here we are here, in marble and gold, did I say gold, yes I said gold, in marble and gold and where—
(A silence)
Where is where. In my long life of effort and strife, dear life, life is strife, in my long life, it will not come and go, I tell you so, it will stay it will pay but
(A long silence)
But do I want what we have got, has it not gone, what made it live, has it not gone because now it is had, in my long life in my long life
(Silence)
Life is strife, I was a martyr all my life not to what I won but to what was done.
(Silence)
Do you know because I tell you so, or do you know, do you know.
(Silence)
My long life, my long life.

Curtain

SOME FURTHER DIMENSIONS
OF STEIN CRITICISM

THERE ONCE WAS A FAMILY CALLED STEIN

GERTRUDE STEIN RAFFEL

Gertrude Stein was my aunt. As far as she was concerned, she preferred nephews to nieces, so I saw very little of her after my childhood, and after she went to live in France.

Nevertheless, I know some things and I remember some things about the "family called Stein", and about the earlier Steins from whom we all descended, for the earlier Steins were my people, too. Our common ancestor was the first Michael Stein, who came to America from Austria in 1841, married Hanna Seliger, and settled in Baltimore. They produced a vast number of children and grandchildren and great grandchildren of whom I am one. One of their sons was Daniel, Gertrude Stein's father and my grandfather. Daniel Stein married Amelia Keyser (whose brother was Eph Keyser the Baltimore sculptor and whose sister married into the photographing Bachrach family) and from this marriage came the Stein family that makes the art history books today:

> "There once was a family called Stein
> There was Ep, there was Gert, there was Ein.
> Ep's sculpture is punk, Gert's poetry the bunk
> And nobody understands Ein."

Well, all that was spoof, because of course the Ep and the Ein were not *our* Steins at all but Epstein and Einstein. And of our Steins only Gertrude made her way into poetry, whereas the Stein family I am talking about consisted of *five* Steins: Michael, Simon, Leo, Gertrude and Bertha.

This article is what I know and remember about those five, before and after the ones who went to Paris became famous, and the ones who stayed home didn't. It's all part of the same story.

First of all, the famous three—Michael, Leo and Gertrude—had exactly the same background as the stay-at-homes and the rest of us. "Business in Baltimore", as Gertrude later wrote about it, was the wholesale clothing business which occupied Michael Stein and his various sons for a good thirty years after coming to America. Business connections with Europe and skill in financial matters led two of the sons to establish a banking and brokerage house in Baltimore, another to enter banking successfully in New York. Daniel Stein, Gertrude's father, stayed with the clothing business for a while but left Baltimore to settle first in Pennsylvania, and then after a European interval in Vienna and Paris, to move west to California. This is why Gertrude's earliest memories were of Vienna and Paris, and why her early adolescence was lived out in Oakland and San Francisco. Of all the brothers, Daniel, my grandfather, was the most choleric, the most restless, and the most moderately successful. He became interested in street-railways in San Francisco but didn't have the temperament for easy success. Both he and his wife died in California in the late 1880's and the early 90's, leaving the rambunctious third generation of Steins behind them, "reasonably poor" as Gertrude put it, and under the care of the eldest brother, Mike. So the "family called Stein", which had moved to California from Baltimore and Allegheny, Pennsylvania, well before the turn of the century, ended up to be a family of orphans.

How each one went from there I'll try to tell.

Michael Stein (1865-1938)

Mike Stein was remarkable. He had been in the street-railway business with his father in San Francisco. When Daniel Stein died, he became the acknowledged head of the family. He somehow managed to liquidate the family debts and turn my grandfather's estate into something sizable enough to let them all do pretty much as they pleased for the rest of their lives.

When things were settled, he married Sarah Samuels, the daughter of a San Francisco rabbi. Before long they'd moved to Paris where Sally soon became well known as one of the early Christian Science practitioners, and then as an early enthusiast of modern art, particularly championing Matisse, with whom she studied for many years. Matisse did portraits of both Michael and Sally Stein which are now in San Francisco.

The Michael Steins maintained a Saturday night open house at their first apartment on the rue Madame, formerly an old religious building which they filled with Renaissance furniture and Matisse paintings. Here many Americans, including American painters like Alfred Maurer, Maurice Sterne, Pat Bruce, Walter Pach, Morgan Russell and Marsden Hartley visited them and were properly amazed at the avant-garde atmosphere and good hospitality they experienced there.

Later on Mike and Sally commissioned Le Corbusier to design a new house for them. It was a great cube of a house with inner ramps and ultra-modern lines. The Renaissance furniture and the Matisse paintings held their own there until Mike and Sarah were drawn back to California again before World War II and it all went to Palo Alto with them to live in a great Victorian house.

Mike and Sally's only son, Allen, grew up and remained in France, Gertrude Stein's intended heir. Allen's son, Daniel, went to California with his grandparents, inherited their pictures and estate, and continues to live there, a writer like Gertrude, and a horse-fancier like his Parisian father.

Mike always remained the shadowy but patriarchal figure of the family until his death in 1938. A full understanding of the five Steins and how they developed would probably show that Mike and Sarah supplied the background of stability and the creative understanding which allowed each of the Stein kids to fulfill themselves so completely in their own way.

Simon Stein (1868-1906)

Every family, I guess, has to have a "funny one." Simon was it. My grandmother's diaries from the California years clearly show he had to be treated differently from the rest. He was enormously fat and was given reducing baths. At times he was not promoted at school. He had to have private English tutoring. For a while the family considered sending him to a special military school.

Gertrude tells how he took Leo's violin out to the barn to make it smell of manure. Leo tells in *Journey into the Self* how Simon took his bow and arrow and refused to return it. He was like that. Not very bright. His interests were practical. He loved to work with the scroll saw. By the age of fourteen he was learning a trade at the Fulton Iron Works.

So, in his late adolescence, Simon took on the practical but not very demanding work of being brakeman and conductor on the San Francisco cable cars. He used to dream that by mistake he'd given twenty dollar gold pieces away instead of nickels for change.

Simon chose to stay on in California when the rest of the family went East. He remained enormously fat. He died in the earthquake and fire of 1906. The family was quick to forget him.

Bertha Stein (1870-1924)

Gertrude did my mother a disservice when she wrote in the *Autobiography* that she never liked her because she ground her teeth at night. Actually, my mother was a person in her own right, although Gertrude and Leo gave her very little credit. They wrote her off because of childhood memories. It was my mother who became the official cook and housekeeper for the family in San Francisco after my grandparents' death. She was a domestic person, little troubled by the divine discontent that shot Leo and Gertrude out of America and into the avant-garde world of Europe.

Bertha liked to cook and run the house and this she continued to do when she moved to Baltimore with Gertrude in 1892. The Bachrach house where they lived had three generations under one roof—lots of aunts, uncles and cousins living in comfortable prosperity as Gertrude described them in *The Making of Americans*. Bertha and Gertrude played duets on the piano, the boys played the violin when they came to visit. Music was always an important part of my mother's life.

When she married my father, Jacob M. Raffel, and had children of her own, she took us all to concerts at the Peabody Institute, and to operas and the ballet throughout our early years. She was well educated and the darling of Uncle Ephrim, who used to take her with him to tea at the house of Henry Walters, the great art collector of Baltimore. My mother lived in a world of flowers, music, cooking and baking. She personally did her own shopping for the house, even after she could have telephoned her orders. She went to market on Tuesday and Friday, and on Thursdays she went in her car to get fresh vegetables, fruit and eggs from the farmers outside Baltimore. Mother lived by the clock and everything had to be on time.

My father was a bright man. He invented a process for making corrugated paper boxes and was very successful at it. We had everything we wanted until his death in 1918. He was a religious man. My mother wasn't accustomed to religion but she had to learn.

Bertha and Jacob Raffel (it used to be Rafael, but got changed when a sign painter spelled it wrong by mistake) had three children, of whom I am one. There were also two boys, Daniel and Arthur. Daniel, a biologist and zoologist, has won many scholarships and lived in many parts of the world. Now he lives on a Maryland farm. Arthur, an electrical contractor, still lives in the Baltimore suburbs. We have all done well by Baltimore.

I was sent to the Park School, one of the first progressive schools. I would only draw. I drew my way through Park School, through finishing school, and then through art school in Baltimore. When Leo Stein was in America, he encouraged me to continue with my paintings.

I had forgotten about Gertrude Stein all those years she lived abroad. Once, when I was a child, she had come to the door to see my mother and I heard the maid say, "There's a lady come to see you. She looks like a gypsy." That was Gertrude. My mother never talked about her for years. Finally, I saw a poem of hers in *Vanity Fair* and I got curious again. Then my brother met her in Paris and she was interested in him because he was intellectual. Arthur met her, too, but she wasn't interested in him. Or in me, when I met her during her American lecture tour. I wrote her several times but I never got an answer.

My mother never wrote to Gertrude. In fact, Bertha never talked about her relationship to the other Steins at all. After she died in 1924 we all had our own lives to live. It was only after a good deal of living and some time around World War II, that I became aware of Leo and Gertrude again. By that time they were internationally famous. I often wonder what Bertha would have thought of that and what they both would have thought about her in later life. What Gertrude and Leo wrote about my mother wasn't flattering, but she was a wonderful person anyway.

Leo Stein (1872-1947)

In 1892 when the west coast Steins scattered, Leo went directly to Harvard. He was first interested in history. Gertrude followed him there and settled in to study at Radcliffe near him. They were very close at the time, Leo Gertrude's closest companion, first guide in reading, book collecting, and aesthetic experiences. Then Leo went to Baltimore and studied biology at Johns Hopkins. Travel, museum visiting, and his acquaintance with Bernard Berenson led him to summer in Europe, in Italy, and then to settle in Paris at the turn of the century.

His own aesthetic experiences began early, in California. He drew. He played the violin. He kept a scrapbook of magazine illustrations. He kept up with local painters like Toby Rosenthal, liked the work of J. G. Brown, the panorama of Gettysburg. He developed a theory of "pictorial seeing" which he later elaborated in his *ABC of Aesthetics.*

Raymond Duncan knew Leo in California when he was impressed by Millet's "Man with the Hoe." He knew him in the early days in Europe (after a round-the-world trip) collecting brass, Dutch tiles, and Japanese prints. Later he absorbed the great master works of the Louvre, and became interested in Italian quattrocentro art and in Goya.

Renaissance furniture was his passion until he heard Berenson discuss the work of Cézanne. This catapulted him to Paris, and soon Leo was buying Cézannes, Matisses, Picassos, and the works of other vital new painters.

By this time Gertrude had given up the idea of practicing medicine and was beginning to think about becoming a writer. She went to join Leo in Paris at 27 rue Fleurus, a place suggested to them by Ephraim Keyser, a Baltimore uncle and well known sculptor who was then living for a year in Paris.

Sally Stein, with Michael's approval and Leo's urging, was already beginning to acquire her big collection of early Matisse paintings. Leo was a natural "explainer", and his enthusiasm for the new painters was very convincing. Now Gertrude found it exciting to join in the hunt for pictures which had the qualities Leo extolled. A second salon soon developed at 27 rue Fleurus. The great trick for the "in group" on Saturday nights was first to go to Mike and Sally's for sedate conversation and good food amongst the Matisses, then to go on to Leo's and Gertrude's where the atmosphere was a bit more Bohemian and the pictures and artists and guests more varied. Leo explained to anyone who would listen. Gertrude played hostess, and slowly developed the critical opinions of her own which finally cut her off from Leo.

The Saturday nights have been well described by Leo in his *Appreciation: Painting, Prose and Poetry*, by Gertrude in her *Autobiography of Alice B. Toklas*, and by Alice Toklas in her *Things Remembered*.

Leo moved out of 27 rue Fleurus after Alice Toklas came to live with Gertrude Stein. With him went the Renoirs, most of the Matisses and Cézannes. He gladly left the Picassos to Gertrude, having lost his interest in that artist by 1912.

Leo had a hearing problem which marked his whole life. He talked incessantly so he wouldn't have to listen. This made a teaching career practically impossible for him, although he tried teaching in America during World War I.

He returned to Paris in 1920 and there, after a painful period of psychoanalysis, he married Nina Auzias. He gradually withdrew from Paris life, becoming a critic and writer and painter. Leo and Nina moved to Settignano, Italy, where they lived until his death after World War II. They had no children.

Leo was a perceptive critic—one of the first to recognize and extoll the genius of the poetic American painter, Louis Eilshemius. As a painter, he was never satisfied with his own work. In later life he lost interest in most of the newer French painters he had championed, except Coubine.

His published work is not extensive, but shows his ability to pursue very advanced, philosophical reasoning. In 1927 *The ABC of Aesthetics* came out. It was intended to be a "popular book" about art. It wasn't, although today Leo Stein's ideas are still quoted. He was ahead of his time. Twenty years later he wrote *Appreciation,* interesting for its version of the 27 rue Fleurus days in comparison with Gertrude's. A rangy book of letters and essays came out in

1950 after his death, *Journey into the Self*. This gives a fuller picture of his tortured self development and the terrible isolation of his abstract mind.

Leo always remained in close contact with New York cousins, Fred and Beatrice Stein. They helped Leo and Nina through the difficult war years and saw to it that Leo's last work was posthumously printed. He always visited Baltimore when he was in America. We thought he was a rather sad and uncomfortable man. I see now that he and Gertrude had this terrific capacity for abstract thinking. In my grandmother's diaries I find Leo and Gertrude linked together by the quality of their minds—even from their childhood: "Leo and Gertrude are honorably promoted, at school, May 21, 1885." This appears over and over. They were a pair.

Gertrude Stein (1874-1946)

From her birth to her death, Gertrude is the one we know the most about. Whenever my grandmother's diaries say "Baby", she means Gertrude. Gertrude had a charmed life as the youngest one in the family. She was coddled and protected. Her mother writes in her diary in Paris when Gertrude was four and recovering from a sick spell, "Gertrude thank God she is better", and "Thank God the Baby is all right again". Her brothers and sister cooperate to buy a canary and a cage for her birthday. She is photographed in Vienna as a "Bayern Maedchen." In Paris her fifth birthday present was a "box of toy furiture." Dresses and hats and gloves were bought for her before the return to America. In California her life was one of reading, family fun, and successful school work. She played the piano well enough to do "Martha" as a duet with her sister. On Thursday, January the 14th, 1886, when Gertrude was only sixteen, her mother writes, "Gertrude weighs one hundred and thirty-five pounds." This same large girl entered Radcliffe nearly a decade later, and hired a boy to box with her every day to get some of that weight off. My mother remembered Gertrude walking in the winter in Baltimore with her coat held open because she was so warm from all that weight. It was not unbecoming. She was round, roly-poly, and angelic looking.

I can't tell anything very special about Gertrude because she has written best about herself—in *The Autobiography of Alice B. Toklas, Everybody's Autobiography, Paris France* and *Wars I Have Seen.*

I can only say that when I saw the beautiful opera *Four Saints in Three Acts* in New York in 1934, the great beauty of the text and the music and the costumes and settings was for me a thing apart. It was only topped for me when, sometime after her death, I heard her last opera *The Mother of Us All.* In the very last lines Susan B. Anthony sings in the opera, I could see that Gertrude was summarizing her whole life, from the time as a child when she wanted fame to the time in her life when she had tasted success and wondered what it was doing to the character of her work.

All her manuscripts are at Yale Library, and they will be a gold mine of information about her and her period as time goes on.

Whenever I go to book stores now I ask for her books, many of which are now available in paperback. The bookdealers always say her work is hard to keep in stock because it is so widely bought by the young.

When I was in Europe after the war, I went to see Alice Toklas who had been Gertrude Stein's secretary for over forty years. She gave me a beautiful tea and told me a story about how when Gertrude gave her great portrait by Picasso to the Metropolitan Museum, and it was about to be shipped, Picasso came to her apartment to take a last look at it. He bowed his head and recited the prayer for the dead. The second time I went to see Alice Toklas she was not anxious to see me. She had grown old and tired and lonesome without Gertrude. She said I had no right to use Gertrude Stein as part of my name. She adored Gertrude and wanted her all to herself. In her *Things Remembered*, Alice B. Toklas writes touchingly of her life with Gertrude Stein and Gertrude's death in Paris in 1946. I am sorry for the younger generation who will never know, except through the force of her writing, about the vital personality of Gertrude Stein. For she was vital. And in this way she really was the mother of us all.

So, "There Once Was a Family Called Stein"

This is the way I, Gertrude Stein Raffel, from my own point of view, see the Steins. Today I walk down the street in New York and see how a syndicate has bought Gertrude Stein's art collection for the Museum of Modern Art for three and a half million dollars, and it will be shown there in January 1971. A big catalogue will be done, and the last word will be written on the Steins and they will be history.

They are already history for me—not just family, but I see where they fit in the history of things too.

They become family history for me slowly. There were the early childhood memories—Leo and Gertrude coming to the house in the early days, Mike coming when Allen was a little boy around 1906. Leo's books coming out after my mother's death, then Gertrude's *Autobiography of Alice B. Toklas* which explained to me what went on with her during all those years between the wars. When she came to America for her lecture tour she became real to me again. I was introduced as Bertha's daughter. Gertrude looked unusual to me—short hair, heavy, as all the family was, except Leo. Then there were my grandmother's diaries which added to the family history for me. They were for the years 1878 to 1885 and my mother inherited them. I sold them to the University of California at Berkeley where they belong now. Those diaries show the daily activities of the Steins as children in Europe. In Vienna: school for the children, visits to Schoenbrunn, the Prater, museums, and flower shows; piano lessons, skating, visits to photographers, and seeing the arrival of the Shah of Persia. In Paris: walks on the boulevards, shopping, the Exposition of 1878, the Louvre, opera ("Freischutz" and "Romeo and Juliet"), ballet ("Leda") and theatre ("Ruy Blas").

Then the diaries show something about the subsequent California life of the family: reading, sewing, gardening, skating, hunting, fishing, swimming, theatre going ("The Black Crook", "The Rag Baby", "Eighty Days Around the World"), drawing lessons, trips to Woodward's Gardens in San Francisco, to the Mercantile Library, and then just walks in the countryside around East Oakland. It sounds like an ideal, free-wheeling life for children.

I began to research for myself. I found again the houses in Baltimore where the family lived. I found the houses in Pittsburgh where the family lived. I found the house in East Oakland, the Stratton place, where the Duncans lived next door to the Steins.

Then I collected all the books Gertrude wrote and all the clip-

136

pings about her work. I saw the two operas Virgil Thomson wrote to her texts. Her complete works are now published by Yale. It seems to me that Gertrude, of all the five Steins, really achieved fame.

Now I see that the Steins are not just *my* family but a family of history. Mike and Simon were a part of California history, Bertha and all her pleasant family living was a part of Baltimore history. Leo and Gertrude are more. They are a part of 20th century international art history, as important in their way as Eadweard Muybridge and Isadora Duncan (both Californians of the same generation as the Steins) became in theirs. Their way of thinking was big. Their way of living and doing things was big. Out of this bigness, at a time when being conservative and with the crowd was a safe virtue, they connected up with the advanced ideas that were in the air of their time and brought them forward, gave them a new kind of form, stamped the mark of their own strong personalities and minds on them.

The open-houses the Steins held in the rue Madame and at 27 rue Fleurus attracted the avant-garde people of Europe and America, and the avant-garde artists, too. Everybody was treated equally by the Steins, for they had learned about freedom and equality on the California coast. Everybody ate well at the Steins, for they had learned about the tradition of Southern cooking in Baltimore. Out of their easy camaraderie and the intellectual ferment they created, came the recognition of the modern movement in art from Matisse and Picasso on. Mike and Gertrude and Leo supported the artists and bought their pictures at a time when nobody else would. They soon got others buying, like the Cones. If you have seen the Cone collection at the Baltimore Museum you will know how the Steins influenced that. If you know the history of the great New York Armory Show of 1913, you know that the American painters who went abroad to organize it went immediately to the Steins for advice and help. Sally Stein showed Matisse paintings in San Francisco as early as 1906. Leo Stein stood up to Berenson after Berenson turned against modern art. Leo became an early theorist about the modern movement. Gertrude did for the English language what the French painters did for French painting. It must have been a lonesome task. Only in her very last few years did she achieve recognition for the power of her literary abstractions.

Now, looking back over the last twenty years since the last of the five Steins died, I propose we rewrite the Stein Song this way:

"There once was a family called Stein
Father Daniel sired no Ep or no Ein,
But Bertha a homebody, Simon a nobody,
And Mike, Leo and Gertrude who shine."

GERTRUDE STEIN AND THE TWENTIETH CENTURY

DONALD SUTHERLAND

Gertrude Stein is said to have said once that there have been only three originative Jews—namely, Christ, Spinoza, and Gertrude Stein. Her companion, Alice Toklas, did not believe she really made that remark, but I still think she very well may have, because of the rather peculiar inclusion of Spinoza in the triad. Why, for so intensively and consciously contemporary a mind as Gertrude Stein's, should Spinoza, of all people, crowd out such figures as, say, Freud and Proust and Einstein? I asked Miss Toklas if Gertrude Stein had really had so high an opinion of Spinoza, and she replied, "Not so high as to read him." Well, the answer to that is that Spinoza is pretty thoroughly unreadable unless you are deeply interested in technical theology, but this does not prevent anyone's knowing that some of his major ideas or intuitions are quite relevant to Gertrude Stein and to much of the twentieth century.

One idea in particular I should like to consider in relation to Gertrude Stein's writing and her view of the world, as well as to the arts of the twentieth century and even to politics. Spinoza argues very simply that since God is a single infinite substance, all things are in God. That is to say that since God is infinite He stops nowhere, not even at matter and evil, and nothing can be excluded from Him. One may refuse the proposition as rank pantheism or as too trivial a turn of logic to swing the realities of experience, but it implies both an ontology and a vision of the world which are of

139

the utmost importance to us. If all things, literally all things, large and small, good and bad, if all things are in God, then they all share equally and directly in final Being, or if you like they are all equally sacred and equally important, all equally and indiscriminately divine presences. I do not feel this way about everything, and most probably you do not either, and it does take a special gift or a special mentality to sustain such a feeling more or less constantly, but such a mentality can be found, not only in Spinoza but in certain Christian saints, remarkably in two of them who were favorites of Gertrude Stein's—Teresa of Avila and Francis of Assisi. It is told of Saint Teresa that when her nuns objected to kitchen duty as beneath their calling she rebuked them, saying "God moves among the casseroles." Or words to that effect. And as it was said of Spinoza that he was drunk with God, it could be said of Saint Francis that he was drunk with fraternal affection for all of God's creatures and creations, not excluding even bodily death, which he called our sister. Gertrude Stein had a good share of this kind of feeling or vision. Let me tell two anecdotes to that effect.

In the summer of 1939, when war was impending, we were sitting in the garden of Daniel Rops, Gertrude Stein's neighbor near Belley, and we were, most of us, getting very depressed over the possibilities of the war, and how in the world, if the world was at all fit for human habitation, could such atrocities as we imagined be possible. And Gertrude Stein said, "Oh yes, I know all that, but to me the world is very beautiful." In strength of conviction and love of the world, this is not unlike Saint Francis's praise of bodily death.

One more anecdote, which has meant a great deal to me, but the point of which is not easy to convey. When Gertrude Stein came to lecture at Princeton thirty years ago, I was a student there and was invited to a reception for her in a professor's house along with a good many other students. Naturally she sat and talked while we hovered and milled about her, most of us in an agitated and awkward adolescent way. Suddenly she made a little sweeping gesture out in front of her, and said, "How is one to describe all this?" All this was disconcerting, because there was nothing in front of her but a casual bunch of Princeton boys, who, I thought, were scarcely worth describing, certainly not as we appeared just then. Perhaps we would have been worth describing separately, in single portraits, or doing something more significant or dramatic than just milling about, and perhaps our inner adolescent lives might have been worth describing, but all that was plainly not what she meant by "all this." What she meant was the immediate phenomenon before her, the actual group as it moved and composed itself and made noises before her, that for her was adequate subject matter, the phenomenon or thing which, like all other phenomena or things, was, so to say, in God. If God moves among the casseroles he may also move among a group of Princeton boys, unlikely as that may seem.

The association of Gertrude Stein with certain saints is real enough, though one can make too much of it. After all she was not a Catholic, not formally at least. Let me tell one anecdote about that, and I shall get back to ideas. In the Fall of 1957 Alice Toklas suddenly announced that she had become a Catholic convert, or rather returned to the Catholicsm of her girlhood after an absence of many years. This made things difficult, since I am an atheist, and it did not make things easier when Alice Toklas claimed I was largely responsible for her conversion, because in the summer when we were vacationing about I had taken her to a very beautiful and very ancient Byzantine or Carolingian little church, Germigny-les-Prés, and the grace of conversion had reached her through the beauty of the building. But one gets used to one's friends being converted and one tries to be nice about it, and when I saw Alice Toklas again I rather egregiously tried to assure her that there was no great incoherence between her belief in Catholicism and her belief in Gertrude Stein, since the Catholic ontology based on Being was not unlike the doctrine of Being and essences implied and explicit in the work of Gertrude Stein. I was rather tiresome about it. I expatiated. She finally stopped me by saying that she had had to announce her conversion to Picasso, too, with some trepidation, because as a Communist he ought to be a dogmatic atheist and not patient with Catholic converts. But he was very nice about it, and when she asked him what Gertrude would think of her return to the Church, he said, "Oh, she was there long before you." In some ways this is true, and very like Picasso to say so in so round and short a way. But there are other traditions besides religion which brought Gertrude Stein to her sense of the equal value of all phenomena. Poetic fervor of a kind can replace religious fervor in sustaining such a sense—you find it very evidently

141

in Walt Whitman—and even the scientific attitude can sustain it, since for science all phenomena are equally in existence, all equally fact.

The most decisive influence on Gertrude Stein in this direction —a mixture of science, psychology, and philosophy—was certainly William James, her favorite professor at Radcliffe. The extreme openness and hospitality to all things which underlies the Pragmatism of James and even directs it articulately, is plain enough, but it was a great pleasure to me to have this connection made very definite by Dr. Haas's publication of the interview with Gertrude Stein, in which she said that James had said to her that the minute you refuse anything, that is the beginning of the end of you as an intellectual. Along with James, or perhaps more *through* James, is the influence of Whitman, on whose pantheism and ecstatic all-embracingness I need not elaborate.

I asked Alice Toklas what Gertrude Stein had thought about Whitman, and she said, "Gertrude thought there was nothing wrong with him except that he was over." Well, these days Whitman is far from over, but perhaps he was over for Gertrude Stein, and in any case his literary influence on her, given his very different sense of words, would have been slight, but his spaciousness of mind, which contributed to that of James, may well count as an influence on Gertrude Stein. And finally there is an influence which I cannot trace very clearly but which may have been strong, that of Santayana, another professor of hers at Radcliffe. As secretary of the Psychological Society at Radcliffe she invited Santayana to speak to the group, but how far his ideas had come along at that time, or how far they influenced Gertrude Stein, I don't know. But his doctrine of Being and of Essences, though carefully schematized, includes practically all phenomena, as largely as James or Spinoza, and even his thought as a young man may well have gone to reinforce the inclusiveness of James for Gertrude Stein, and perhaps even induced a linear precision and Spanish hardness into the rather high and nineteenth century eloquence of James.

But it is high time for me to illustrate by quotations how this mixed tradition—philosophical, scientific, poetic, religious— comes out in the work of Gertrude Stein. This is from *A Long Gay Book*, an early book of considerable interest though of incoherent form, as it makes the transition between the style of *The Making of Americans* and that of *Tender Buttons*. But you will recognize it as fairly typical Stein, and if you will also remember the traditions behind it which I have been describing, I think you will feel how exalted and passionate, as well as how precise, an expression it is.

> *Loving is something. Anything is something. Babies are something. Being a baby is something. Not being a baby is something.*
>
> *Coming to be anything is something. Not coming to be anything is something. Loving is something. Not loving is something. Loving is loving. Something is something. Anything is something.*
>
> *Anything is something. Not coming to anything is something. Loving is something. Needing coming to something is something. Not needing coming to something is something. Loving is something. Anything is something.*

And later in the same work:

> *Anyone being one is one. Anything put down is something. Anything being down is something and being that thing it is something and being something it is a thing and being a thing it is not anything and not being anything it is everything and being that thing it is a thing and being that thing it is that thing. Being that thing it is that thing and being that thing it is coming to be a thing having been that thing and coming to be a thing having been that thing it is a thing being a thing it is a thing being that thing.*

I asked you to notice in that passage, or those passages, the lyrical and caroling quality, the lyricism of ringing the changes on a single idea, as for example a litany would have it, and I do hope you got the hang or the ring of it; but now I want to treat in a very pedantic or scholastic way the fine distinctions that Gertrude Stein, as a student of philosophy and as a very committed intellectual, makes between *a* thing, and *anything*, or between *something*—as we would say in the vernacular, something that is really *some*thing—and *any*thing, or as we would say in the vernacular, something which is just anything.

I don't know whether anybody but professors of philosophy can be interested, at this time of day, in Duns Scotus, a thirteenth century philosopher who was, oddly enough, the great inspiration not only of Leibnitz, who is in vogue again, but of Gerard Manley Hopkins, who has had a huge influence on the English poetry of the twentieth century, though not on Gertrude Stein. The importance of Duns Scotus to us, through Hopkins or not, is in his theory of the *species specialissima,* or the terminal entity of any immediate phenomenon, the peculiar character of which, in unique conditions of space and time, cannot be dissolved away into its component general forms, such as yellow, small, alive, animal, and so on, or its inclusion into a class, such as Bee. Scotus called, or presumably he did, this very individual character or specific quality of any concrete phenomenon, its *ecceitas*—or its there-it-is-ness—or again its *haecceitas,* its this-here-ness. This insistence on the immediate individual thing as a final reality, as final as general ideas, or even the featureless reality of Being Absolute or Being itself, is if you like a traditional problem, but I think it has never been so real in experience as in the twentieth century, when the individual has become as it were absolute, and at the same time the collectivity of individuals into a more or less coherent mass has become more imposing and practically imperative.

Let me give you an example of this problem in a passage from Gertrude Stein, not in full. There is a rather famous passage in a work called *Useful Knowledge*—and the word Useful is not altogether a joke—where she counts up to one hundred by ones. It goes, one and one and one and one and one and one and one and one and one and one and one, and so on mercilessly until the announcement that we have reached one hundred, I hope you see how crucial this is, that in the collectivity of one hundred, each of the things which are absolute ones to themselves, are perfectly respected and not lost in the accumulations of quantity, such as two or three or forty or seventy-five or whatever, until we get to the total. The equal insistence on the integrity of each component part is a very important twentieth century thing, obviously in politics, but even more evidently in the arts. I could easily remind you that Gertrude Stein grew up during the feminist movement, which proposed that woman were equal to men, and Gertrude Stein finally

144

decided that children too should have the vote, since they have equal stake in existence with adults, but the point is that the group or the family, especially the patriarchal family in which the individuals are severely subordinated to the group, is transcended for a view in which all the component individuals are absolute existents to themselves, and compose if at all a total of integers formed by all of mankind taken not as families, nations, classes or whatever, but as a sum of equal individuals. I shall not insist on this, but in spite of the formation in our century of elite or minority groups, in spite of the struggles in politics which exploit majorities and minorities, we do, deep in our hearts, have a strong feeling of the equal existence and of the right to an individual existence, of each and every one in the world. I don't think that this feeling has ever in history been so basic or strong as in the twentieth century, and indeed the counter-movements, Fascism and Communism, which respectively try to subordinate an unindividualized mass to an undividualized minority or to subordinate all individuals and groups to a homogenized majority or totality, do nothing but try to change the more obvious twentieth century conviction that one and one and one and so on make one hundred, not cumulatively or in such proportions as twenty and eighty, but one by one by one by one.

Let me put it this way, very directly. If you say one and one are two, do you absorb the essential singularity of the ones into the group of two or do you not? In marriage, where one individual and another one individual are joined in a couple, do we any longer feel that the one or the other one is essentially a component of a couple or dyad instead of a single absolute unit, or do we not? I think that in people we now count by units instead of by groups, and that the family is no longer convincing. Nor larger groups, like the party, the class, or the nation itself.

So, one and one and one and one and one and so on. A Spanish poet once wrote that the angel of numbers goes from the one to the two, from the two to the three, and indeed it does take a supernatural power like an angel to sink one unit and another into a duality, and a duality with another unit into a triad.

Let me apply this to painting in the twentieth century. One of the major accomplishments of Cézanne was precisely the assertion of the equal existence of each or millemeter of his canvas with the existence of every other inch or millimeter. With Cézanne this is not a dramatic exaltation or subordination of certain parts of the picture over others, though they do, as we say, add up to a total. No doubt the origin of this in Cézanne was in part the impressionist movement, or the pointillist movement, in which every spot of color was an equally important and equally scientific optical or retinal event, but Cézanne made objects and shapes, not merely events, into an equally emphatic existence in equilibrium over his whole canvas. The Cubists took this up too, the equal diffusion of geometric shapes over a whole canvas, with no dramatic focus or culminating point. Parallel to this would be the care with which Rousseau painted each leaf of his trees, one by one, neglecting the collective bunches of foliage which say Corot had painted. And even now, with Mondrian or Mark Tobey or Pollock, we have gone on with his equal emphasis of visual events or shapes over a whole canvas, an equal tension if you like, though of course there are other theories and practices of composition.

What I mean may be clearer if I discuss something many of you may recently have read, *The Banquet Years,* by Roger Shattuck, which was recommended to you, and with reason, since it is a magnificent work and delightful to read as well. But Mr. Shattuck, though not unreasonably, takes issue with me on a distinction I made, in my book on Gertrude Stein, on the difference between a prolonged and a continuous present, and the difference is rather to the point I am now discussing. I did not make myself very clear, I am afraid, in the passage Mr. Shattuck quoted, but what I more or less meant was that a prolonged present asserts a theme and then proceeds to complicate and elaborate it, in the manner of say a fugal theme in Bach, so that the presence of the original theme, no matter how elaborately overlaid with variations, is maintained or prolonged as a going existence in each present passage or moment. It is as if one counted one two three four five six and so on, where the original unit of one is prolonged and present in the other figures in which it remains a component. But a continuous present, I think I meant, would be one in which each unit, even if identical or nearly with the previous one, is still, in its present, a completely self-contained thing, as when you say one and one, the second one is a completely present existence in itself, and does not depend, as two does or three does, on a preceding one or two. One and one and one and one. In this case, each one is a completely separate assertion of a complete entity and is not prolonged from the preceding unit or units, but comes as a new thing, and each one arrives in a continuous present, that is, the present is so continuous it does not allow any retrospect or expectation, as when you say, in such counting, two, you look backward to one and forward to three, or even more. You must also be aware of the most notorious sentence of Gertrude Stein: A rose is a rose is a rose is a rose. In this case, we have not a consecutive counting but a moment by moment insistence on the rose, and each moment of insistence is a heightened and refreshed recognition of the rose, not merely a prolongation of the rose, as could perfectly well be done in another era, as Goethe might have said to the rose, *Verweile doch, du bist so schoen*, even if the prolongation meant his damnation.

That is one way of feeling about things, and indeed the way I mostly feel, that things should if possible be prolonged to my present experience if I love them, but I think the twentieth century thing is certainly to take each present moment with its content as an independent and absolute event, even if the content has occurred before. One and one and one and one. Gertrude Stein came to thinking and saying that there was no such thing as repetition, since each time the thing or word recurred the insistence was different or new. And if one counts one and one and one and one, you might say that none of the ones is the same as any other, and if asserted as a complete thing in a continuous present, it does not look backward to a previous one or forward to another one to follow. Hence, in a modern composition of this kind, each part or moment or instant is complete in itself and does not proceed from anything else or look forward to anything else, and in the total they are as it were simultaneous, as when counting one and one and one and one and so on, the total of one hundred is simultaneously, not cumulatively or gradually, arrived at by all the units together. This may remind you of Leibnitz and his monads, which are mutually impenetrable units, absolute to themselves, but united in a preestablished harmony, like clocks set at the same hour and synchronous, under a total or arch-monad which is God.

Well, never mind Leibnitz. After all, philosophy does not justify anything in the arts, even if in a way it clarifies, and bringing in philosophy can be depressing. It should not be, but it usually is, so I shall stop it, and remind you instead of certain quite practical features of the twentieth century world which correspond to the sort of composition I am discussing. One evident feature is our extraordinary mass-production and series production, the assembly line and so on. It is still possible to have a custom-made car or a custom-made suit, but why bother—the normal thing is to have a car or a suit which is exactly like thousands of others from the same company. This worries some people, as if their individuality were at stake, but in fact if you have say a new Mustang it is your own Mustang, even if it is not fully paid for, and you go your own way in it and treat it as if it were unique. And even if there are thousands of suits exactly like the one you are wearing, it is still your suit, you are by yourself in it, and you make the particular creases in it all by yourself, the way it hangs on your posture is all yours. That thing is being that thing and not being just anything it is everything—that is, it is everything to you if you are fond of clothes and like the suit or dress you are wearing.

Another twentieth century thing which is getting progressively more insistent is the sky-scraper, all the stories of which are getting more purely identical, with less use of subordinate groupings or blockings in the facade. And apartment houses are much the same. They horrify some people, but they are more and more just that, one and one and one and one endlessly, and still, if you live in one and are living an intense private life inside it, this very identical apartment has to your experience a quality all of its own, it becomes independent and even quite disconnected from all the others like it. Subjectively and intensively speaking, that is, while objectively and extensively the units are progressively more uniform. Someone, I think it was Frank Lloyd Wright, called our huge apartment buildings and housing developments slums or tenements for the rich. Well, that is very interesting, that the rich and the middle class and the poor should all be living in much the same way. We still have zonings and brackets and Negro sections and Chinatowns, but really the distinctions are pretty well disappearing, with some violence and resistance, it is true, but disappearing all the same. You may or may not like it, but there it is.

The principle of this kind of composition is very aptly called by Mr. Shattuck juxtaposition—as against subordination or progression—what in grammar we call parataxis, eminently the dominant syntax in Gertrude Stein, not to mention Homer and the Bible, with which works she grouped her own. In this style things are associated, as she said, "so nextily." But there are, as Mr. Shat-

148

tuck points out, two very distinct ways of composing in juxtaposition—first the juxtaposition of nearly identical though independent units, as in one and one and one and so on, and second, the juxtaposition of things that are very different in kind and quality. Gertrude Stein shifted from a style in which things were simply alike to a style in which things are simply different, so she put it, and she made the change in the course of *A Long Gay Book*. Let me read a passage from the later phase of that book, in which the juxtaposed elements are "simply different."

All the pudding has the same flow and the sauce is painful, the tunes are played, the crinkling paper is burning, the pot has a cover and the standard is excellence.

At least two important things can be said about this. One is that in any given immediate scene, no matter how commonplace, there is bound to be an association of disparate elements, which exist very vividly to a perception persuaded of the equal importance of all phenomena, even if they are largely irrelevant to the main gist of the scene. Instead of letting things go at "I had a good pudding with sauce piquante for supper" she gives an equable list of concomitant phenomena, some relevant, some not, to the main practical event, but all of them equally and simultaneously existing in perceptual fact. The written composition, made of the disparate elements abstracted, has certainly a strangeness, if you like a senselessness and lack of meaning, because it isolates or detaches from a perfectly commonplace or generic and generally recognizable event like having supper those elements which made it a special and unique event, which made it not *a* thing but *that* thing, those elements which make up its *species specialissima*. Here of course we run into difficulties, and the famous obscurity of most of Gertrude Stein's work after 1911 or 1912, since anything has meaning, that is, has a recognizability, by virtue of belonging to a general class of phenomena, such as having dinner, and here we have the subject presented, not exclusively but predominantly, by those elements which distinguish or separate it from its class. So you see what she must have meant at Princeton. She could have said, "I spent an evening with a bunch of Princeton boys," but that would not have described the unique immediacies of what she saw and heard before her.

149

Anyway, when she writes of unique immediacies and suppresses the generic element, one is always or nearly always tempted to puzzle it out, to induce or restore a generic element which will make the composition "comprehensible." But immediate experience in its real immediacy is not comprehensible, has no meaning, and when you do induce a meaning you falsify the essential immediacy. Gertrude Stein once remarked, "What is strange is this" —meaning that this thing as this thing is new and unfamiliar, as this thing it exceeds or comes loose from the class to which it belongs, from identification and identity so to say.

Now is this a twentieth century thing or not, a thing existing in its unique immediacy and not by its participation in a class of phenomena? I think it is. Let me give you a painful example, the assassination of Mr. Kennedy last year, followed by the murder of Mr. Oswald. Admittedly the whole weekend was both superb and intolerable; everyone, under the impact of those strange immediacies, surely lost several pounds of weight, as I did, and surely we all tried madly to explain what it was about, to get some sort of meaning into it. And one attempt was to classify it, we were reminded that presidents are assassinated, and we counted off Lincoln, Garfield, and McKinley, as if that more or less accounted for Mr. Kennedy.

And then there was the question of conspiracy, whether it was a Communist plot or a heavily disguised Fascist plot, or again just a result of the social and psychological forces at work in Mr. Oswald's case history. Well, one did try to escape from the tragic immediacy into classes of events and into causalities, but these escapes were surely much less interesting than the immediate events themselves, and by now, surely, nobody is much interested in how or why it happened. Some intellectuals, it is true, of the kind that insists on figuring everything out, are still disputing the matter, but I think the public at large simply treasures the event itself, the albums of photographs, so to say, rather than any possible explanation. Well, not that art in the twentieth century has the intensity of an assassination, even if the Surrealists tried to make it that way, but it can very well and usually does exist in disconnection from any reference or extrinsic meaning, by the beauty or intensity or character of its immediate properties. As one may say that the almost but not quite appropriate color of Mrs. Kennedy's dress is more intrinsic to the essence of the assassination than the political reasons for the event. Even if there are reasons, and of course there must be, the quality of most events in the twentieth century, whether in public or private life, whether in art or nature, is to be quite arbitrary and disconnected from everything else, to be, as it were, *something*. Our venture of getting to the moon, for example, has such very feeble reasons, such as the idle curiosity of Science, that Mr. Kennedy was quite right in saying simply and roundly, "We *choose* to go to the moon." And now it appears we are not stopping at the moon, but going straight on, for no explicit reason at all, to Mars.

What makes all this very different from the nineteenth century is that the nineteenth century was still interested in causes and purposes and explanations. It was dominated, if not by Evolution, under which everything, even if incomprehensibly, served some future purpose or other—contributed in some way to "some far-off divine event toward which the whole creation moves," at least by a sense of direction in History, whether Hegelian or Marxist or what not. In my younger and more Leftist days I used to think that the twentieth century sense of arrest in history, the suppression of the movement of time—as in the continuous present of Gertrude Stein or the substitution of relatively timeless forms like geometry by the Cubists for the temporal and optical events of the nineteenth century Impressionists—was a sort of bourgeois conspiracy to arrest the dialectic of history while the Bourgeoisie was more or less on top and in its element. One may perhaps still think that, and even think that the extraordinary domination of the scientific world by physics instead of biology—that is by an eventful but non-progressive science instead of one which was essentially a study of gradual growth upwards—has been a bourgeois conspiracy or at least a bourgeois intuition, but I do not in the least, at this time of day, take this kind of opinion seriously. Partly because politically it can reverse itself. The cause of the Negro, which in the nineteenth century could be thought of as committed to a gradual evolution, as slow as the development of new species in animals or plants, is now evidently advanced in the immediate manner of physics, as a sudden and constant movement, not a gradual one. The Negro has ceased to wait. And who does wait, now, for anything? And the reason we do not wait is simply that we no longer believe that things are progressing of themselves, and of course we have become quite habituated to the idea, under the bomb, that not only

151

biology but human history itself can end at any moment. Thus we live, oddly enough, in a continuous present, in which nothing is felt to lead to anything else, because at any instant there may be nothing left for it to lead to.

After the first World War, which made it clear to the more sensitive members of civilization, that progress had been a delusion, and that individual existence was so expendable that it could not count on more than a span of a few days, and after the second World War, when the two nations of Europe which had a certain reputation for intense civilization, that is, Germany and Italy, showed themselves the most atrociously barbarous, with indeed the participation of certain elements in England, France, and America, and of course Spain, the whole question of history as something with a meaning, much less a value, came surely foremost.

In literature, and I shall mean mainly American literature, we have had a very interesting split, between those who still cling to history as a valid dimension for human habitation, and those who reject it. The school of T. S. Eliot and Ezra Pound is evidently of the twentieth century, but with their everlasting historicism, their infatuation with tradition, which they set against the going present for the most part, they are still not weaned from the superstitions of the nineteenth century. But any century includes, as part of its full character, an opposition to its major thesis, so one may say that the rear-guard action of historicist writing and art is still component to the essence of the century. Not only that, but now in 1964, when the present events are so demanding on the imagination, and hit the sensibilities with so violent a shock, it is natural that a great many people should try to find a ground of assurance or of perspective in the past.

The present, continuous or not, is a good deal too much, so that even the presumably most contemporary poets tend to take up Buddhism, a very ancient state of mind, or, as with Charles Olson, the oldest American history, or, as with innumerable young poets, descriptions of Renaissance Italian monuments. Henry James once called Europe the great American sedative, and indeed the European cultural past, and now the Asiatic cultural and religious past, have become the refuge of the nervous American against the arbitrary and miraculous violence of present events, when the recourse is not to actual intoxicants like peyote, marihuana, or alcohol.

152

Well, it is all very tempting. Gertrude Stein was determined, in her time, to stay with the twentieth century, come what might, but only in her art. For personal comfort she sat amongst Renaissance furniture, a devotion to the Republican Party, and fundamentally the moral views of a lady of 1902. We all need some sort of ballast for navigating the present, some distance from which to see it straight, some still point or continuity from which to measure or count off the chaotic events of the moment, but at least Gertrude Stein used her residual nineteenth century habits as a personal comfort, while as an artist she could risk taking on the twenieth century directly. She used to say that the twentieth century in the arts was created by America, meaning herself, and by Spain, meaning Picasso, but that it had to be created in Paris or rather in France, because France afforded a traditional and unchanging ground upon which or against which to erect the twentieth century compositions in writing and painting. That is the way she felt about it, and it may be more generally true, that France has not created much of the twentieth century, though she has been immensely present at it and exploited it well enough and refined it, in her painting at least, and her literature remains extraordinarily academic and traditional, even and most hilariously in Jean Genêt.

But to stay with American literature. As I said, there are the culture people, after Pound and Eliot, who not only use the past as a recourse against the raw violence and disconnections of the present, but prefer the past, and use it as a contrast and reproach to the present. Nevertheless, we have many writers committed to the present, without benefit of either a cultural heritage or so dubious an arrangement or prearrangement of values as is available at a price in the Catholic Church, or the Communist Party. But in a general way those writers and poets who do maintain the raw or unhistoric present do not get much beyond notation or documentation, that is, the bare recording of a passing impression or of how some group lives, whether urban hipsters or garden suburbanites or the oppressed. In short we are falling back on nineteenth century Naturalism; even if the writing is more violent, the content and the vision are strikingly those of the nineteenth century, of Naturalism, all over again. The innovations of form are very minor indeed, not much more than a bleaker or a more florid manner than usual.

For several years now it has been regularly said that the period of innovation in the twentieth century, so far as the arts are concerned, is over, and this may or not be a good thing. Good or bad, it may be natural and inevitable, not just as a reaction but as a maturation. Gertrude Stein used to compare the life of a century to any human life. In a century's youth it is naturally in revolt against the older century in order to establish a life of its own; it sows its wild oats and goes a little wild, but once it has won the struggle to lead its own life it calms down, becomes mature and civilized in its turn, enriching and refining the main attitudes of its youth and even affecting the mannerisms of its parent century.

Before she died Gertrude Stein came to feel that the twentieth century was unduly prolonging its youth, that it was time for it to slow down a little and behave itself, or simply enjoy itself. In a way one is tempted to agree; one would like a certain amount of tranquility in the Arts, just to offset the increasing violence of the real world. And such a comforting or consolatory art is indeed not alien to twentieth century art from the beginning.

You may have noticed in Mr. Shattuck's book the intention of Matisse to make paintings like armchairs, and of Satie and his group to make a music like furniture, as if it were an agreeable environment rather than an exciting series of auditory events. One may, especially from the French point of view, read the twentieth century that way, and one may even adopt the French point of view in the interests of civilization and pleasure; but I do think that from the American point of view and from what was once a Spanish point of view, one cannot go against the intrinsic energy of the century, its splendor, its violence, its savagery if you like. One may certainly try to transcend it, but one cannot, as a serious artist, or as a serious beholder of the Arts, content oneself with something which is not in on the essential realities and energies of one's time in the real world, or really enjoy something which is an evasion or a refusal. Interfused with the pleasure principle, as Freud called it, there is the reality principle, and though the two may conflct, I do think it is true that any assured and full and confident pleasure has to rest on some adequate satisfaction of the reality principle. So far so good, and it is easily said, but what is not so easy is our present difficulty, the incoherence between the violent or intensely realistic content of much contemporary writing and the fundamentally placid and unventuresome form in which it

154

is expressed. And after all, in art the expression is everything, and the form is everything to the expression—at least I feel not only strongly but ferociously about this, being a professor of Greek and Latin, lo these twenty-five years.

Before getting to my point, let me make sure I am not misunderstood in connection with Greek and Latin. My classical training and profession, which you might think would exclude me from an interest in Gertrude Stein, commits me first of all to a very minute concern with words, an endless and almost pathological patience with their meanings, which is required for reading Gertrude Stein as it is for reading Homer; and second, and much more important, a quite fanatical belief in rhetoric, not in the least as a set of rules for correct writing, but as the indispensable source for adequate expression in words of the quality of the subject. The inventiveness of the Greeks and Romans as well in finding adequate formal tropes for the quality of anything they found themselves called upon to express is what has kept me at them all these years, and though many other things attach me to Gertrude Stein, what really holds me is her overwhelming rhetorical agility with the perfection of each syllable of her wording—perfection again not in the sense of being correct according to some high school standard of good writing, but in beauty of calligraphic poise and shape and a tight fullness of meaning, exactitude if you like. Perhaps I am still being pedantic, no doubt I am, but with the differences I have just described. Though Gertrude Stein announced often that she was a grammarian, I would go a little farther than grammar and say I value her also and most as a rhetorician. To a rhetorician, for example, there is no difficulty whatever in "A rose is a rose is a rose is a rose."

So now, to the point; her rhetorical resources were for the most part equal to expressing the quality and composition of the twentieth century reality as she intensely and devotedly experienced it, and that reality in her experience was conditioned not only by a hyperacute perceptivity but by an enormously broad and endlessly subtle intelligence, which took on the totality of the world—excluding nothing as I said at the beginning.

I cannot tell, just now, whether she is back in fashion again or out of fashion, as she recently has been except for a scattering of devotees, but I am quite persuaded, that if our present problem is to be solved, namely finding a rhetorical adequacy of expression

155

for the essential realities of our time, the way things are and the way things go and the way things connect with each other or do not, Gertrude Stein will have been the great predecessor, the great teacher too in some degree. The literature I hope for will be sustained, as hers was, not on a literary or cultural tradition so much as on a minutely tuned and perfected verbal instrument, a radically philosophical intelligence applied to words and things alike in their most vivid aspects—and then, finally and most important of all, on a passion for the world. It can be a happy passion, or a tragically unhappy passion, but it has to be a quite unreasonable love for this disastrous and very beautiful world.

About the Contributors

ROBERT BARTLETT HAAS is Director of Arts and Humanities Extension at UCLA. He is the "Berkeley Bobbie Haas" of *Everybody's Autobiography*, and appears as "Bobolink" or "Bobchen" in other writings by Gertrude Stein. Editor and Prefacer of *What Are Masterpieces*, recently reprinted with fragments of "Gertrude Stein Talking" as an Afterword, he has for many years catalyzed Gertrude Stein activities on the West Coast. By 1940 he had read all the unprinted work of Gertrude Stein in manuscript, and his fifteen years' correspondence with Miss Stein has been put on permanent deposit at Yale.

GERTRUDE STEIN RAFFEL, the daughter of Gertrude Stein's sister, Bertha, is a painter in her own right and a collector of Stein memorabilia in New York. "There Once was a Family Called Stein" was written to coincide with the exhibition of the Stein family collections, "Four in America," at the Museum of Modern Art.

DONALD SUTHERLAND's book, *Gertrude Stein: A Biography of Her Work* set the pace for serious Stein criticism in 1951 and has not been surpassed to date. Mr. Sutherland first presented his paper "Gertrude Stein and the Twentieth Century" at the University Conference Center at Lake Arrowhead in August, 1964. His view of the twentieth century he shares with Roger Shattuck, but the dimensions along which he sees Gertrude Stein are uniquely his own. Mr. Sutherland is listed in the *Directory of American Scholars*, and is Professor of Classics, University of Colorado.

157

Acknowledgments

To Mr. Donald Gallup, Curator of the Gertrude Stein Collection, Yale University Library, for help and encouragement.

To the Estate of Gertrude Stein, Baltimore, Mr. Daniel C. Joseph, Administrator, for the following: "Ada", "Ladies' Voices", "Portrait of Mabel Dodge at the Villa Curonia", "Susie Asado", from *Geography and Plays*; "Advertisement", from *Lucy Church Amiably*; "A Movie", from *Operas and Plays*; excerpts from "The Mother of Us All", from *Last Operas and Plays*; excerpt from *Brewsie and Willie*; two "Radcliffe Themes", from *Gertrude Stein: Form and Intelligibility*, by Rosalind Miller; "To Bobchen Haas", from the estate of Alice B. Toklas.

To Oxford University Press, for the excerpts from *Gertrude Stein In Pieces*, by Richard Bridgeman.

To Pitman Publishing Corporation, for the following: "A Saint In Seven" and "Identity a Poem", reprinted from *What Are Masterpieces*, by Gertrude Stein.

To Random House, Inc., for the following: "Picasso" and excerpts from "Tender Buttons", copyright 1946 by Random House, Inc. Reprinted from *Portraits and Prayers*, by Gertrude Stein, by permission of the publisher: "Valentine To Sherwood Anderson", "An Elucidation", "George Hugnet", "Portrait of Mabel Dodge", copyright 1934 and renewed 1962 by Alice B. Toklas. Reprinted by permission of Random House, Inc.: specific excerpts from *Everybody's Autobiography*, by Gertrude Stein; from *Lectures In America*, by Gertrude Stein; from *The Geographical History of America*, by Gertrude Stein; from *The Philosophy of William James*, edited by Horace Kallen.

To Yale University Press, for excerpts from *Gertrude Stein: A Biography of Her Work*, by Donald Sutherland.

158

DATE DUE